Praise for

The Outdoor Table

"Alfresco eating at its freshest and most colourful. I would love a seat at Alanna's outdoor table."
— Paola Bacchia, author of *Istria*

"Alanna O'Neil's *The Outdoor Table* is more than a cookbook; it is an immersive masterclass on outdoor entertaining, with practical tips on everything from lighting to food safety. The simple, fresh recipes, designed to be prepared in advance, are a delight for the eye as well as the palate. I will undoubtably use this book as inspiration for all my outdoor meals in the years to come!"
— Laurel Evans, author of *Liguria*

"With recipes and pairings that are as gorgeous as they are delicious, *The Outdoor Table* will completely change your next alfresco meal. Full of bright and vibrant photography, Alanna inspires you to step outside for your next meal, bring together friends and family, and enjoy some of the most beautiful plates. She takes you beyond the food with so many helpful tips and inspirational ideas for taking your next outdoor dining experience to another level. *The Outdoor Table* is an absolute must-have addition to your cookbook collection."
— Lisa Dawn Bolton, author of *On Boards*

The Outdoor Table

For permission requests, please contact the publisher at:
Mango Publishing Group
2850 S Douglas Road, 2nd Floor
Coral Gables, FL 33134 USA
info@mango.bz

For special orders, quantity sales, course adoptions and corporate sales, please email the publisher at sales@mango.bz. For trade and wholesale sales, please contact Ingram Publisher Services at customer.service@ingramcontent.com or +1.800.509.4887.

The Outdoor Table: Recipes for Living and Eating Well

Library of Congress Cataloging-in-Publication number: 2022933218
ISBN: (hardcover) 978-1-64250-856-7, (ebook) 978-1-64250-857-4
BISAC category code: CKB082000, COOKING / Tablesetting

Printed in the United States of America

The Outdoor Table

Recipes *for* Living *and* Eating Well

yellow pear  press

CORAL GABLES

Contents

"COOKING AND EATING FOOD OUTDOORS MAKES IT TASTE INFINITELY BETTER THAN THE SAME MEAL PREPARED AND CONSUMED INDOORS."

—FENNEL HUDSON

AN OPENING NOTE

I've always felt that cooking and baking are some of the warmest gestures of love, kindness, and hospitality. Whether it is slicing up an oven-fresh, steaming loaf for an impromptu visit from a friend, making a dish for an intimate weekend dinner party, or sharing a good home-cooked meal, cooking and baking are gifts to those you love most. I am just a home cook, merely equipped with years of trial and error and a deep love for cooking and baking. Often, I find myself up to my knees in a rather challenging or complicated recipe simply because I enjoy the process and presence it requires, even if I'm left alone with two dozen flaky croissants. Whatever I make, even if it's a little higgledy-piggledy or a touch brown, I love to share it as much as I love to make it. There is nothing quite like sitting down to a plate created with thought, love, and care. The pleasure of inviting friends and family over to share a beautiful meal isn't meant to be perfect or rigid. I simply don't live or entertain that way. Apart from the winter months, our ceramic table on the terrace is surrounded with friends, family, and anyone else we can squeeze in for a sunset dinner under the twinkling lights. Good food is meant to be shared, and it's as simple as that.

Sharing a meal outside makes the occasion even more unforgettable and special. Growing up, we always had a rotation of friends and family coming around for outdoor dinner parties, whether sitting on the front porch for a midsummer barbecue or a bowl of fresh blueberry cobbler with a front seat to a summer lightning storm. When I dine at a restaurant, I usually choose to sit outside without a second thought, unless it is intolerably cold or hot. There is something inexplicable about dining outside. I can't quite put my finger on it, but I've concluded it's a stimulating medley of sensory feelings of sights, sounds, tastes, and touch. The sun seems all the brighter, the breeze gentler, life feels slower and carefree…and the food is more colorful and enticing! It even seems to taste better; perhaps the fresh air or sunlight adds some magic to the dish. Maybe it's the little bird that cocks its head curiously at you on the chair across, waiting for a crumb of your bread. Everyone seems to linger over the table a little bit longer, engage deeper in conversation, and savor the moment.

I've always been an outdoor enthusiast and spend as much time as I can adventuring in nature. It's my place of solace and comfort. I truly believe that living well with a happy mind and heart is deeply intertwined with our connection to the natural world. I'm the sort that will happily plop down in a sunny spot on the porch steps in mid-winter with my breakfast. It breaks up the daily routine adding a little bit of joy to what might be an otherwise dull day. Sharing a meal outside enriches our relationships and enhances our quality of life. Life just *feels* more alive! Sharing a meal to the hum of the bees, chirps of the birds, or rhythm of the waves, makes life seem simpler and joyous…as it should be. How important these little things are to our well-being and contentment. We remember the gatherings that remind us to live in and cherish the moment. And what a privilege that is! It is filling in more ways than one. Living and eating well, I believe, begins with embracing our roots in nature and our connection to each other. With thoughtfulness and a little planning, the outdoor table is a great place to start.

How to Use This Book

The word "entertaining" feels a bit too pretentious or showy for the outdoor table. In my mind, the outdoor table is a true, generous display of warmth, hospitality, with a little merriment in the mix. It should be gratifying not only for your company, but also for you. An outdoor gathering tends to be more casual since being exposed to the elements leads to the possibility that anything could happen. When it does, we must put up our hands, relinquish control, and go with the flow. The wind may blow away your napkins or the mosquitos may decide to snack on you, but I hope this book addresses these little details with good taste and simplicity. And more importantly, to provide you with tempting, easy-to-make-ahead dishes and menus so you always have something up your sleeve at the ready. This is not a lavish book with three- or four-course meals, fancy china, and handwritten place cards. Rather, this book is meant to inspire you to invite friends over for a relaxing and lighthearted occasion full of conversation, laughter, sunshine, stories, and of course, good food.

Just like there is no one way to host a relaxed dinner party outside, there is no right or wrong way to use the recipes in this book. I provided some menu suggestions at the end of the book, but you can pick and choose based on your tastes, mood, and guests. Think about what you enjoy serving, what's in season, and what works for you. Perhaps you skip a main dish and serve a plentiful spread of tasty appetizers and two or three light sides or fresh salads. There is no need to stick to the standard starter, salad, sides, main dish, and dessert courses. You can, of course, but don't feel pressured to cover all these bases. A generous and delicious spread is bound to be a success regardless. I prefer a hodgepodge of delicious food that has an atmosphere of "let's dig in" and "pass the wine." Serving in this style naturally evokes a relaxed and easy ambience. The weather and season will also dictate what I might serve. For instance, if it's exceptionally hot and humid, I would keep the menu light and cool. I would opt for dishes that require a mere matter of assembly and perhaps forgo firing up the grill altogether. That may seem obvious, but there have been too many occasions where I've got carried away imagining an exceptional dinner menu only to be melting in the heat left with only an appetite for something ice cold. Use your instincts and do what's right for you and what works for the given occasion. These back-pocket recipes are meant to be easy to throw together, "a little of this and that" type of cooking style for a backyard gathering. They also can be easily doubled if needed and are meant to be intuitive and flexible. When the weather is sublime, I don't particularly enjoy spending all day in the kitchen fiddling away with intricate or time-consuming recipes. My hope for this book is that it makes outdoor entertaining a delight and relaxing, where everyone is invited and wants a seat at your outdoor table.

ALANNA O'NEIL
PO BOX 727 MAKAWAO HI, 96768

THE INVITATION

"Eating outdoors makes for good health and long life
and good temper, everyone knows that."
—Elsie de Wolfe

The start of a lively and fun dinner party is an enticing invitation. Before you begin your preparations, having your guest list roughly sorted out, considering the possibility of one or two tagalongs, is where to start. Decide how many people you can reasonably host and, more importantly, have the energy to entertain. Sometimes an overflowing cheeseboard, a crusty baguette, a simple salad, something bubbly, and vanilla bean ice cream with fresh strawberries and cream can be more than enough for a splendid lunch. Having more guests doesn't necessarily mean more work, but it will take a few tricks and techniques to accommodate a larger group. At least you will have more hands to help wash up! Regardless of the number of people you'd like to invite, the most important thing to consider is making it feasible and enjoyable for you. Trying to do too much will inevitably make you feel overwhelmed and disheartened. To avoid unnecessary stress, rally up your guests for a headcount so you can prepare accordingly.

If you're planning for a weekend gathering, send your friends and family a tentative invitation a week in advance. I say tentative because it depends upon the weather as well. A proper invite allows you plenty of time to prepare around the forecast. The summer months are naturally more suitable for outdoor dinner parties and celebrations, but passing thunderstorms may be quite common where you live. Broadly speaking, you can host throughout the year, not just in the summer months. I love to host an autumnal gathering, cozied up with blankets, wooly sweaters, and all. A gooey butternut lasagna with the backdrop of vibrant leaves is a gorgeous way to celebrate the season. If the forecast looks bright and promising, confirm with your guests it's a go. If the weather does turn last minute, you can always take it inside.

Even if you are hosting the gathering at your home, invite your guests to bring a dish or dessert. An outdoor potluck is a wonderful alternative to making every dish yourself. It may be even more festive with an abundant array of delicious options to pick and choose from. Don't hesitate to delegate out dish ideas, especially if you're hosting, to close family and friends. It may not be suitable for some occasions, but it can relieve some pressure and stress, especially if it is a bigger gathering or celebration. Whatever hosting style you choose, the intention should be to create a lighthearted, breezy, and tasteful gathering that will leave your friends and family looking forward to the next invitation.

A GOOD HOST

Being a good host is at the core of all entertaining, whether it's a glamorous cocktail hour or a Sunday backyard barbecue. It is a skill that can be cultivated and gets better with practice and willing company! Even the most casual lunch can be thoughtful and gracious. As a host, you set the mood and atmosphere of the occasion. It should reflect your personality, while still being attentive to your guests. It's a dance that starts the moment they walk in the door, as the queen of etiquette, Emily Post, asserts. Greet them with a warm smile or hug, offer to take their coat or belongings, or make them feel comfortable with a refreshing cocktail or drink. What truly makes a gracious host is considering every guest individually, even down to the little ones, with thoughtfulness and kindness. With genuine warmth and thoughtful courtesy shared throughout the evening, your guests will head home with a smile on their faces and lightness in their hearts.

Naturally you may have a few last recipe steps to finish, but creating an easy, light, and happy air the moment they arrive takes the pressure off you from the start. Sometimes making a joke or finding humor in a disastrous situation, such as a recipe gone wrong, or a toppled cake can set everyone at ease. Preparing as much as you can in advance is the key to a smooth, relaxing, and fun gathering. You should enjoy it as much as your guests, especially after all the effort and care you've put in! By working out all the little details beforehand, when your guests arrive, you can greet them graciously. You can lead them to the terrace and chat without feeling frazzled or overwhelmed. I love to catch up with my company in the sunshine with a refreshing cocktail in hand before sitting down to eat. After all, when friends and family come around, spending time with them is what it's all about. And the food shared should complement that, not be a burden.

SET THE SCENE

Like an idyllic painting of a golden sun shining in cornflower blue skies with billowy clouds, creating a beautiful scene is just as important as planning out an enticing menu. There is something so welcoming about a thoughtfully set table outside. The dappled sunlight dancing on the linen and the breeze ruffling the blooms on the table creates a scintillating atmosphere. Even if I'm serving something simple with close family, I still try to make it look pretty and inviting. My view is that setting a lovely table doesn't inherently make it feel more formal or stuffy but rather makes for a more enjoyable and memorable occasion. Because at the end of the day, you set the flow and feel of the meal. I like things to feel lived in, not uptight or sterile, especially when entertaining outdoors. It doesn't take much effort either because half of the ambience is already created purely by being outside! Although you don't necessarily need all these items below to create a splendid table or evoke a convivial feel, collecting a few will entice you to have friends come 'round for a sunset dinner more often.

The Outdoor Table

An outdoor table is a place where memories are created, stories are told, and good food is shared. The table is a place to gather. Whether it's a picnic table in the backyard or a wrought iron table out on the lanai, finding a table that suits you and your style is the foundation of all great dinner parties, lunches, cookouts, and anything in between. Usually, I find that longer, rectangular shapes fit more people and are easier to shift around if needed instead of something circular. It doesn't necessarily have to have matching chairs or be an expensive set. Honestly, I prefer something that looks a little more worn, weathered, and rustic. Those kinds of chairs and tables have character and feel more inviting. It feels like old memories are seemingly etched into them. Sometimes I simply pull out a spare table from inside the house and set it up for the evening under the trees. Any rugged or stained table can be transformed with pretty, pressed linen into something lovely. If you're in the market for an outdoor table specifically, look for something weatherproof. For seating, scour estate sales, antique, or charity shops for mixed match chairs or farmhouse style benches to add a charming touch. Have extra chairs on hand too, so you will always be able to accommodate that extra plus one.

In Maui, summer can be extremely hot, leaving you feeling like you're melting away like the ice cream cone in your hand. Try to position the table in the shade if possible, or under an umbrella or awning, especially if you plan to dine midday. Overall, food doesn't fare well under direct sun exposure for a long period of time either.

Linens

There is nothing quite like crisp linen. A fresh, pretty tablecloth or runner can easily makeover a rather nondescript and shabby table. I like to choose something light and neutral in color, such as sand, stonewashed gray, cream, white (of course), or a pale blue. Small floral patterns in a pale or neutral color can be quite charming and demure. Otherwise, I find patterned or large floral prints to be quite distracting and jarring, although if you love it, go for it. (I am partial to neutral stripes—must be that New Englander in me!) Likewise, with napkins, I prefer neutral linen or cotton. You can find lovely affordable handmade options on Etsy or thrift shops. Buying up a few sets in different colors or even small patterns will brighten up the table. I like to have a variety to play with, especially if some get worn or stained after a rowdy dinner party. Also forgo paper ones if you can, especially for a Friday dinner party with a few friends; they just don't feel special or add any substantial quality to the overall feeling of the evening. Reusable napkins are also a more sustainable option. For a big barbecue or a larger get-together, rather than having a pile of saucy, stained napkins to wash on repeat or spot-treat the following day, use a durable yet attractive alternative to paper. They are thicker, feel like napkins, and will go much further than those flimsy, nearly sheer standard ones. Lastly, for a laid-back weekend soirée or lunch, fancy table accessories aren't necessary. Casual outdoor entertaining for me is less about the trimmings and more about a relaxed and beautiful ambience with good food and good friends.

Lighting

One of the easiest (and inexpensive) ways to set the mood or atmosphere of a dinner party is with some glow and sparkle. Light is ethereal, inviting, and enchanting. In the evening, scattering a few tea lights around the table or lanterns on the deck instantly creates an intimate and warm ambience. I like to use sturdy clear holders, Moroccan tea lights, and votive glasses. Mason jars (again the do-it-all wonder) also make practical tea light holders and add a rustic touch. Clusters of candles of varying heights down the table can be quite alluring. Torches, either flammable or LED, staked around the perimeter are both celebratory and practical. For those pesky uninvited guests (mosquitos), include a few citronella candles around the perimeter and on the table in the buggy summer season. What I love in high summer, especially on a warm, balmy evening, is lingering under bistro lights. Lights have a way of transforming an otherwise uninspired setting into something festive and special.

Serveware, Plates, & Glasses

Most of what you use day to day is perfectly appropriate for outdoor dining, especially for intimate gatherings, but I would be mindful of using anything too precious or fragile. In Maui, the trade winds are an ever-present factor to consider. I can't tell you how many times the wind has knocked over wine glasses, flower vases, and scattered napkins every which way. A word of caution not to use your prized showpieces from the cabinet or something you couldn't part with. Accidents happen, be it natural, pet or child related! So, with that in mind, I opt to use mismatched transferware sets found on Etsy or at a thrift shop for a nice lunch or dinner and enamel for a larger party or barbecue. If any shatter on the stone steps, no tears will be shed over it. They are inexpensive and can be easily replaced. The same goes for serving platters or bowls. Enamel or melamine are lightweight, unbreakable, and available in a rainbow of colors. Do yourself a favor and save your precious porcelain from getting the odd chip or scratch.

An outdoor dinner party wouldn't be complete without something refreshing, be it bubbly or a zingy lemonade. For glassware, I prefer tumblers, mason jars, and stemless wine glasses. (If it isn't windy, I adore those vintage coupes or slim wine glasses). I always opt to use glass when it's practical to do so. In the same mindset of the plates, go with something that won't shatter your heart too. Nowadays they make some fantastic acrylic and shatterproof options that you'd swear were glass. They are far more attractive than the old and dated plastic-looking ones. The handy dandy Mason jar is a versatile and inexpensive alternative to your finer stemware or glasses for a barbecue. Stack or arrange them on a pretty tray by the pitcher or wine for everyone to help themselves. A trusty galvanized bucket full of ice is an appealing and generous display for beer that is an easy step up from a basic cooler. If you have a larger group, scatter a few buckets around the area with ample ice and stocked to the brim.

Blooms & Fruit

Now we've come to my favorite part of setting the table: using fresh flowers, greens, and the season's bounty. If there is one trick that makes a table look instantly welcoming and special, it's this decorative touch. Whether you are hosting five or twenty people, arranging some fresh and colorful blooms is essential, and there is no reason they should be a costly addition. My approach, if you will, is rustic and seasonal. I prefer using what is readily available in my garden or a simple bouquet picked up at the farmers market. If I'm in a pinch, using hearty and lush greenery gathered outside can be quite lovely when done right. It takes only a minute to arrange and is well worth the effort. Be it wildflowers, olive branches, from roadside floral stands, apple or peach blossom branches—all are simple, natural, and beautiful. Whether you pick a sweet confection of May's peonies or cheery, golden sunflowers, be sure to use a properly weighted vase or a pitcher. Little bud vases with single blooms scattered down the table runner can also

be darling and practical, especially if there is a steady breeze. I swear I drive with one eye on the road and another looking for wildflowers, blooming trees, and honesty box bouquets. Setting a pretty table can be effortless. Another gorgeous idea that makes the whole table feel plentiful and inviting is various bowls filled to the brim with ripe, juicy fruit and veggies. With a big bowl of lemons, artichokes, and heirloom tomatoes—*Benvenuto a Sicilia*! Especially in the summer and harvest season, I love to showcase the beautiful abundance on the table. This is a particularly effective decorative trick if it is windy or you don't want anything too tipsy with lots of little ones running around. And why not offer up those just-picked juicy peaches at your feast?

Extra Bits

If you entertain outside often or aspire to, it might be worth investing in some of these bits and bobs. Without a doubt, the summer months can often be unbearably buggy. Flies, mosquitos, and other pesky creatures can be a real nuisance hovering over a beautiful spread and biting your guests. Mesh or cloth food covers can protect your dishes and cheeseboards from those relentless party crashers. Another handy item to have on hand is a utensil holder, either made of wood, rattan, or wicker. It's a tidy and casual way to present utensils and weigh down napkins for everyone. Trays of wood, rattan, ceramic, melamine, and materials of all sorts are great to have in your entertaining armoire for serving cocktails, appetizers, wine glasses, and more. Speaking of drinks, a glass drink dispenser is an attractive way to serve a larger group, especially for water, lemonade, iced tea, and such.

Outdoor Entertaining Essentials Checklist

- ☐ Sturdy table and chairs to seat at least 6–8
- ☐ Umbrella or another form of shade
- ☐ A variety of linen and cotton tablecloths and napkins
- ☐ Plate sets for at least 6–8 people
- ☐ Utensils
- ☐ Utensil holder
- ☐ An assortment of platters, serving bowls, and trays
- ☐ Wine glasses, mason jars, water glasses, serving pitcher
- ☐ Bottle and wine openers
- ☐ Picnic knife
- ☐ Galvanized bucket
- ☐ Tea lights, votives, sturdy candles, citronella candles
- ☐ Sturdy floral vases and bud vases
- ☐ Torches
- ☐ Strings of globe bistro lights
- ☐ Mesh food covers
- ☐ Wine glass tags
- ☐ Lawn games
- ☐ Wireless waterproof speaker

A Brief Note on Cocktails, Cheeseboards, & Appetizers

Before the dinner party is in full swing, I like to designate an area or spot for drinks, cocktails, and any cheese or charcuterie boards. Perhaps I'll pull out a small side table and place it nearby for guests to help themselves to drinks or designate it as the cocktail mixing area. Any coolers or galvanized buckets of beers and drinks can be set on the side too.

For the grazing boards that everyone will be hovering around, I think it's best to place them on another table altogether, rather than the main table. The reason being is that the board can still be picked over while enjoying the main dinner or lunch without taking up too much space on the table. Also, if you are hosting a larger lunch or dinner party, having the cheeseboard or appetizers on a separate table instead of the dinner table emboldens people to mix and mingle. If it's a more intimate crowd, say four or six, having the board on the actual dining table makes more practical sense. It encourages everyone to linger a little longer and chat over it before the meal.

PLAN & PREPARE

Entertaining can feel quite overwhelming, even if it is with the closest of company. For most, the weekends are an obvious choice as it allows you time to shop and prepare. The more time you have to prepare, the more freedom you have to play with the details and perhaps experiment with a new recipe rather than your tried-and-true, dog-eared go-to. Although, that's not to say that weekday gatherings don't have their place. They can be just as casual, fun, and easy, not to mention adds some pizazz to a monotonous work week! When I feel like having company over, I'll peek in the pantry to see what I've got on hand as a place to start. I may or may not use anything I find in the cupboards, but it at least gives me a starting point and some inspiration.

Having a well-stocked pantry gives you a solid foundation to work from when you start planning. Humble staples such as grains, dried pasta, crackers, nuts, rice, dried beans, oils, vinegars, mustards, jams, baking essentials, and various spices will be the beginnings of many wonderful and wholesome meals. A seasonal and flavorful pasta dish with fresh summer veggies is my go-to that can feed a crowd and come together in minutes. You'd be surprised by what you can throw together with a few staples from the pantry with the goodies in your community-supported agriculture (CSA) box, farmers market haul, or garden. A provisioned pantry allows you the flexibility and freedom to not only entertain at a moment's notice but saves time and subverts a potential headache. Crafting a meal with a few pantry essentials takes the edge and pressure off. I like to buy them in bulk if they are high quality and nonperishable. With a little creativity, fresh produce, and a trusty back pocket recipe, pantry staples will make outdoor entertaining breezy and enjoyable.

Another factor to consider when planning out your lunch or dinner party is timing. Before I even begin to play with the idea of inviting people over, I ask myself, how much time do I have realistically? I know that if I don't have the energy to present my best, even if it's simple, I'd rather save it for another day. From there you can use your best judgment of how simple or elaborate you want to get. Perhaps it ends up being just cocktails, tapas, and a generous cheeseboard. When you have more time to prepare and plan, such as a weekend barbecue, map out the timings for each recipe. For example, I try to prep as much as I can before my guests arrive, including chopping, peeling, cooking rice, and baking any bread or desserts the day before. A fruit crisp is equally, if not more, delicious when enjoyed the following day with just a brief touch-up in the oven.

Lastly, another timing factor to consider is to tidy up around your outdoor table or terrace or wherever you plan to serve outside. Birds do fly about, leaving you-know-what on the table, and the kids' toy box may have overtaken the entire deck. It's best to have the dining area neat, relaxing, and clean before anyone arrives. Get the umbrella up and ready, brush off the chairs and benches for any flyaway leaves. The last thing you want to be doing is hosing down the whole patio while your friend sips some wine while simultaneously attempting to block the spray. Take time to set the atmosphere and scene beforehand; it will make all the difference when you get down to cooking. The added effort will make you feel inherently proud and confident about your lovely space and handiwork. If you have any early guests, they can settle into a relaxing and welcoming space with the birds and blooms.

SAVOR THE SEASONS

"I like to think that to one in sympathy with nature, each season, in turn, seems the loveliest."
—Mark Twain

I cherish seasonality. It's no secret—from activities to food. Perhaps it's the anticipation of waiting for that special moment when the cherry tree blossoms or the luscious strawberries ripen; it marks a moment in time to both reflect and honor the present, which is ever so fleeting. The seasons are at the heart of my entertaining style and deeply influenced how I learned to cook and bake. With four (or six depending on who you ask) wildly different seasons in Vermont, it brings both a challenge and excitement with every passing one. When the warmer months languorously roll around (about time) after a long winter, it is a pure treat to celebrate a delicious meal outside with what the season brings. Maui, in its blissful and laid-back island way, further embraces this way of living. I like to view outdoor entertaining through that lens of natural simplicity. During the winter or drearier months of the year, I like to take the time to try out more laborious recipes, heavier roasts, and baked dishes. Although, when the weather is as delightful as a daisy, I tend to keep things simple and let the purity of the season shine. A colorful riot of ripe cherry tomatoes with a dash of good olive oil and salt with a handful of fresh herbs is equally if not more delicious than a painstakingly adorned salad with everything in it but the kitchen sink. Outdoor entertaining should complement the seasons; after all, how could you not be inspired to plan a summertime soirée when the weather is gorgeous? One simple way to showcase the season is selecting one dish, perhaps a salad or dessert, and showcase one ingredient—be it tomatoes, melon, zucchini, or peaches. It is an easy entry to begin to learn how to plan a menu around what's in season and use your senses. Another way to incorporate more seasonality in your cooking is to visit your local farmers market or farm stand. Ask the purveyor what is particularly good at the moment or pick what looks fresh and ripe. Better yet, ask them how they like to prepare those zebra-striped beans! They will be proud to show you, so don't be shy! This will make you savvier when entertaining outside and a better home cook.

On the farm, nearly every summer dinner party out on the porch consisted of a dazzling plate of juicy ripe tomatoes from the garden, heaping piles of basil, and luscious mozzarella with a drizzle of olive oil, balsamic vinegar, and sea salt. Look to the bounty and harvest of the season; be it spring, summer, or autumn, the simplest of ingredients can be elevated into something marvelously delicious and heavenly. It takes very little to dress up fresh greens, veggies, and sweet fruit. That is why, as you will see throughout the book, most of the recipes are based on seasonal abundance, especially for sides, salads, and desserts. With ripe seasonal produce, good extra virgin olive oil, salt, and some seasonings, you're already halfway there. That is the beauty of simple and seasonal recipes; you can play, improvise, and make do with what you have at the ready opposed to trying to make mealy apples appetizing in the spring. Most of the dishes we serve at our family gatherings and summer barbecues are straight from the garden. Alternatively, bring your shopping list to source the best local ingredients at your neighborhood farmers market too.

What makes an ideal dish for an outdoor dinner party or lunch? In my opinion, it is something that takes little preparation and holds the same carefree, just-toss-it-together, throw-it-on-the-grill attitude. Incorporating a few seasonal key players in your dish makes this all the more achievable. When you use the ripest and freshest foods of the season, they don't need much dressing up, as opposed to serving a seemingly decent recipe that would be far better served six months from now. Entertaining with the seasons makes you more of an intuitive cook and host. The spirit of eating outside is just as a sensory and pleasurable experience as the menu itself, so why not showcase the season's beautiful bounty? Getting inspired by what's fresh and overflowing from the garden or farmers market is a good place to start when planning your next gathering at your outdoor table.

A NOTE ON FOOD SAFETY

One important factor that guarantees an outdoor gathering is a splendid success is ensuring that the food fares well outside in the elements. Here are a few considerations to keep in mind when planning your get-together, especially for a larger buffet-style setting. Some of these do apply for even a smaller, intimate gathering so it's worth noting even if you're having a casual dinner out on the patio with friends.

As much as we all adore a leisurely barbecue in the summer months graced with blissful sunshine and cloudless blue skies, bugs and mosquitos love the nice weather too. When serving a buffet-style table, especially on a hot summer's day when pesky insect flocks come out of nowhere, cover the dishes with a light, attractive tea towel, napkin, or mesh food covering once everyone has got their share. It hardly needs mentioning that flies buzzing about your delicious food is not the least bit appetizing or tempts a second helping.

If it is a particularly humid and sweltering day, I like to keep the dishes covered because food tends to wilt, especially the fresh, green ones you would most likely be serving on such a day! Salads, cheeseboards, fruit dishes, and wine do well with a cover. An alternative option is to keep the food set up inside for everyone to make a plate and then head outside.

Cheese should be served at room temperature so it can breathe and relax, but it loses its appeal when it begins to melt and soften into a rubbery wedge in direct sun. If there is a decent amount of leftover cheese from your grazing board, bring it back inside after the meal for snacking or repurpose it later. I hate to waste good cheese, or food for that matter! If possible, place the food under the cooler shade.

Any grilled meats, seafood, cold cuts, or salamis should also be kept out of direct sun. Cooked meat can be safely enjoyed an hour and a half after it is prepared, but even then, I prefer to serve everyone immediately. It looks unappetizing after drying out in the open. Upset stomachs are not part of the program! Cured salamis hold up far better outside than cold cuts or cooked meats but still consider using a mesh cover if you plan on leaving them out for the entirety of the meal.

Desserts and other sweets also don't fare well in the hot sun. I like to bring out the tart or cake just as we are about to eat dessert. Keep anything with whipped cream or ice cream inside until dessert time; you'd be surprised how quickly things melt once out in the warmth of the day, even on the kitchen counter! The dessert recipes in this book have passed the Hawaiian heat test! Although, when in doubt, set it in the fridge or the freezer until it comes time to serve.

STARTERS

A dinner party menu often follows a flow, from appetizers to dessert. I find this more formal than it needs to be, especially for a relaxed Sunday dinner on the lanai. I don't necessarily believe in serving specific dishes to start dinner or lunch. The familiar atmosphere of having friends or family come around doesn't quite fit with the formal courses. Having a rigid first course seems to interrupt the conversation and banter, especially when everyone wants to enjoy themselves and relax with another glass of wine. I prefer simple bites and finger foods that satisfy a crowd so everyone can just dig in. A big bowl of olives, salted nuts, salty kettle chips, dried or fresh-sliced fruit, crisp grapes, or a hunk of good cheese and crackers are all perfectly fine to set out for hungry guests to pick on and chat over while you finish up in the kitchen. By no means underestimate the ease and satisfaction of a tried-and-true briny bowl of olives, grapes, creamy cheese, and a good loaf of bread! Something sweet and savory—that is my basic starter formula in a pinch for a low-key gathering, not a smorgasbord but satisfying enough so you don't spoil any appetites! That is my only real steadfast rule; I don't truly believe in serving traditional canapés, which is why this book has slim pickings of those sorts of recipes. The recipes, such as the Baked Feta on page 59 and Castelvetrano Olive Breadsticks on page 64, in this section are more like accompaniments to the main plates.

Although, when I'm in the mood to make it feel a little more special, I'll include a few simple starters. There are no rules on how many to serve or what is appropriate; you could easily offer both a grazing board and an uncomplicated starter. For a small, intimate group, I may include a cheese and charcuterie board with one or two small starters. Cheese and charcuterie boards are easy to replenish. Present them with overflowing salty nuts, wedges of cheese, and ripe berries. They are ideal for big groups. The less work you can make for yourself in the end, the better while still offering a generous and delicious spread. Less stress and pressure is best! So, when I start to plan for company, I think of what I'd like to serve as a main dish and work backward from there. Any sides and desserts that follow will complement the main dish. You'll find in this section I've included some simple starter recipes for when you may want to take it up a notch. At the end of the day, it's up to you and what you feel like!

Gather & Graze

A generous and hearty cheeseboard is always a good place to start as you finish up bits in the kitchen or the grill. It can all be prepared in advance, which is the key to easy outdoor entertaining. You can sit back and relax with your company and feast away on the board, knowing you don't have to fuss over so many dishes and timings. Who doesn't love to sit outside on a glorious summer day with some good wine and cheese? With that said, I like to keep these two basic attributes in mind when I'm shopping and creating my board: sweet and savory. Think fresh, seasonal fruit or veggies, a trio of ripe cheeses, a variety of cured meats, seeded crunchy crackers or a baguette, salty bits such as nuts and olives, and a few spreads such as honey or grainy mustard. This is the time to raid the pantry! Presentation is everything, and you don't need a culinary degree to make it beautiful, especially when enjoying it outside in a natural setting. You can't go wrong with grazing boards, but don't let your guests spoil their appetite by constantly snacking! Serve the amount that feels adequate for the number of guests so that everyone can have equal pickings. I try not to replenish the board unless someone has clearly hoarded all the cheddar. It should be a bountiful offering but by no means a meal replacement! There is nothing more disheartening than taking the time and care to cook everyone a delicious meal, and then they barely touch the main course due to swollen stomachs full of bread and cheese! As I mentioned, the rules aren't set in stone so, if you are ever so bold, you can entirely forgo any and simply serve the main course in a timely way. If you opt for that route, one thing is for sure: everyone will be hungry! I do what feels right for me and aim for that Goldilocks "just right" balance of serving too much and not enough.

Cheese

When perusing the cheese section, I aim to select at least three different varieties (usually it ends up being a few more; it's hard to limit myself). Firm/aged, semi-firm, bloomy rind, wash rind, blue, and fresh are the basic cheese categories to begin your curation. Ideally selecting one of each creates a well-rounded board. Goat, sheep, and cow's milk are the milk varieties to consider; select at least one of each. Also take texture, color, and richness into consideration, for example, a creamy, gooey brie compared to a craggy blue Stilton and a fresh white burrata. If something looks or smells interesting, give it a try! Life is too short to stick to the same old standbys, especially in the cheese department. Opt for at least a quarter of a pound of cheese per person, although I tend to err on the more generous side as you can always repurpose it. A variety of good cheese can add up in price rather quickly if you are entertaining a large party, so if you are on a budget, don't load up the basket willy nilly. (If that is the case, forgo serving cheese altogether and simply serve a fresh dip such as the Crème Fraîche dip on page 45 with a seasonal crudité platter. A basket of veggies is far more budget friendly then a basket artisan cheeses!) Whichever scrumptious wedges or wheels you choose, be sure to serve them at room temperature. Like wine, they need to breathe and relax; you can cover them with a mesh cover to keep those determined bugs away.

Grazing Board Picks

Vermont or English sharp cheddar
Blue Stilton or Bayley Hazen Blue
Brie
Camembert
Fontina
Taleggio
Burrata

Epoisses
Goat cheese
Feta
Smoked gouda
Parmigiano Reggiano or Pecorino Romano
Extra-aged Manchego

Charcuterie

A variety of salamis and cured meats are a great addition to a well-rounded board. Aim for at least two or three distinct kinds. Many cured meats are seasoned with blends of herbs and spices. Select wines that complement your cheese selection nicely. For example, spicy hot chorizo would be mellowed out by a creamy, mild cheese such as a chevre or burrata. If you are ordering by the pound at the deli, consider at least three slices per person. Don't hesitate to ask your butcher, likewise with your local cheesemonger, for some suggestions and pairing ideas. Olympia Provisions is my one-stop shop for artisanal cured meats. If you have the palate, pâtés, terrines, and other forcemeat can add a luscious and luxurious element to your spread.

Grazing Board Picks

Finocchiona salami

Chorizo

Genoa salami

Soppressata

Capocollo

Prosciutto di Parma

Serrano or Iberico ham

Bread & Crackers

Good bread is one of my weaknesses. Although "good" may be subjective, I must admit I can be a bit of a bread snob when it comes to fresh bread. No matter what I'm serving for a lunch or dinner party, bread is always on the table in some shape or form, either homemade or picked up from the local bakery. It's a sign of hospitality, warmth, and generosity. Quality makes all the difference when it comes to bread. Treat it like a centerpiece. Good bread is just as essential as any cheese or other appetizers. Whether a crusty French baguette, ciabatta, sourdough, lavash, or pita, choose two different varieties with a backup just in case. Slice them up in manageable-sized pieces for your guests to easily help themselves. Likewise, with crackers, offer two or three different kinds for an assortment of texture, crispness, and flavor. I prefer farmhouse-style crisps with all sorts of nuts, seeds, and dried fruit baked in.

Fresh Fruit & Vegetables

Now let's add some freshness and seasonality to the board. First and foremost, I like to use whatever is bright, ripe, and in season. And given that the growing and harvest season is partnered with the warm months of outdoor dining, it is quite easy to do. Look at what's growing in the garden or spilling over the tables at your local farmers market. They are utterly delicious when plucked from the tree or pulled from the ground and are cost-effective, especially as cheese and meats can end up costing a pretty penny for a large group. Overflowing and colorful fresh produce, whether heaping piles of blackberries, vibrant rainbow carrot shards, or plump cherry tomatoes, certainly make even the humblest of boards look exquisitely beautiful and robust. When paired with a fresh and luscious dip, no one will be wondering where the cheese is. Most fresh fruit and vegetables make great finger foods to start, so I like to keep it as simple as possible without much peeling or slicing. Have a balanced selection of both. Oh, don't forget fresh herbs! Basil, thyme, rosemary, sage, and chives are wonderfully fragrant additions to tuck in and around the board. Let the season guide you!

Grazing Board Picks by Seasons

Spring

Raw snap peas
Radishes
Blanched asparagus
Artichoke hearts
Apricots
Kumquats
Grapefruit
Strawberries

Summer

Rainbow carrots
Celery
Broccoli florets
Cucumber
Raspberries
Blueberries
Blackberries
Red or green grapes
Watermelon
Pineapple
Peaches
Plums
Tomatoes of all varieties
Anything growing in the garden!

Autumn

Roasted beets—ruby, striped, or golden
Carrots
Roasted sweet potatoes
Roasted squash
Apples
Pears
Figs
Persimmons
Cranberries

Winter[3]

Pickled beets
Pickled green beans
Dried fruit
Figs
Tangerines
Mandarins
Oranges
Pomegranates

» *3 I included winter since some climates are mild at this time of year and can be cozy if done right!*

Accompaniments

To top off the board and fill in any little gaps, I like to pile on salted or raw nuts, olives, fresh honeycomb, dried fruit, date cakes, and any other sweet and savory bits I may find. Tuck them in and around the other items, letting them spill over which makes it look like a spread fit for royalty. Grainy mustards, honey, chutney, jams, compotes, dips, and preserves are delicious accompaniments to slather on with a slice of cheese and baguette. Pickles, cornichons, pepperoncini, roasted red peppers, and pickled summer vegetables add a briny tang to balance some of the creaminess and sweetness. Use fresh herbs as a vibrant and aromatic garnish too!

CRÈME FRAÎCHE DIP WITH GARDEN HERBS

Serves 6

8 oz (227 g) crème fraîche

8 oz (227 g) whole fat sour cream

Juice of ½ lemon

2 tablespoons chives, minced

1 heaping tablespoon thyme leaves
  (reserve a few springs)

1 heaping tablespoon tarragon,
  minced

1 heaping tablespoon green onions
  (pale end), minced

1 teaspoon kosher salt

Cracked black pepper to taste

Rather than popping open a store-bought dip, this simple dip takes only minutes to whisk together for a crudité or grazing board. It's an elegant addition to serve for a light lunch or with cocktails on a sunny afternoon.

In a small mixing bowl, combine all the ingredients until smooth and creamy. Taste and season with more herbs, depending on your taste. Garnish with a few springs of thymeand minced chives with a good crack of black pepper on top.

SWISS CHARD & CANNELLINI BEAN DIP

Serves 6

2 15.5-oz cans (878 g) cannellini
    beans, rinsed

2 whole Swiss chard leaves, stalks
    removed and roughly chopped

1 garlic clove (2 cloves if you love
    garlic like me!)

Juice of ½ lemon

1 heaping tablespoon lemon zest

4–5 tablespoons extra-virgin olive oil

1 teaspoon kosher salt

Cracked black pepper to taste

2 tablespoons minced lemon rind

This dip reminds me of a vibrant Vermont summer with its verdant hue. It's a fresh and creamy dip that looks beautiful on a colorful grazing board.

In a food processor or blender, add the beans, Swiss chard, garlic, lemon juice, and lemon zest. Pour in the olive oil while pulsing the mix until smooth. You can add a tablespoon of water or olive oil if it's too thick for your taste.

Season with salt and pulse once more.

Scoop out the dip into your serving bowl. Give it a few cracks of black pepper on top and garnish it with the lemon rind and a few bits of minced Swiss chard. I like to drizzle a little more olive on top before serving.

A SIMPLE FRESH SALSA

Serves 6

1.5–2 lbs ripe Roma tomatoes
  (about 8–10), finely diced
¼ red onion, finely diced
2 garlic cloves, minced
1 generous handful cilantro, minced
½ cup (118 ml) extra-virgin olive oil
2 teaspoons white wine vinegar
Juice of one lime
1 teaspoon kosher salt
Optional: 1 jalapeño, minced

A good quick salsa should be in any host's recipe book to whip out when a party calls. Using the ripest and freshest tomatoes you can find at a farm stand or farmers market or in your garden truly makes a difference in taste. Make it as spicy or mild as you like. It keeps in the fridge for up to five days too.

Combine the diced tomatoes, red onion, garlic, and cilantro in your serving bowl.

Pour in the olive oil, vinegar, and squeeze in the fresh lime. Continue to season with the salt and jalapeño if desired.

Gently spoon the salsa together, give it a taste, and season with additional salt if needed.

BRUSCHETTA

This is one tried and true classic—and for a good reason. If I had to choose one appetizer, it would be bruschetta every time. What I love about it is that an ordinary piece of toasted bread can be fixed up into something delicious with simple, seasonal toppings. When you start with fresh and quality toppings, unpretentious bread can easily please a hungry bunch. With endless combinations to create, you'll need something more substantial than standard sandwich bread or crackers. Typically, a hearty sourdough, ciabatta, or baguette is a good place to start; they are sturdy, crusty, and flavorful. I've included three favorite recipes of mine, but the beauty of bruschetta is how creative you can be, or resourceful for that matter! I've hosted many impromptu get-togethers where I didn't have much time to plan or shop. But with a peek in the bread box, I sliced up my day-old sourdough, brushed it with a clove of garlic and olive oil and toasted it on the grill, and topped it with some fresh ricotta, olives, and a few slices of heirloom tomatoes from the garden, and voilà! When it comes to a little bite to eat before dinner, a day-old loaf can go a long way with a few simple ingredients. The toppings—a soft cheese or tapenade—can be as humble or elegant as you like. Look to the seasons for guidance. Juicy heirloom tomatoes from your garden or the farmers market are worth their weight in gold, and with a dash of salt and pepper, they are scrumptious. Grilled zucchini topped with some fresh herbed goat cheese showcases the seasonal abundance. Get creative and try including different textures and flavor profiles together too—creamy, soft, crunchy, tart, sweet, salty, bitter, spicy, and so on. Decisions, decisions!

Once you've chosen your toppings, the most authentic way to serve them is by grilling the bread, either directly on the grill or in a cast-iron skillet. The slices should be about ½" thick, which can be cut in halves or quarters. I like to take a halved clove of garlic and rub it on both sides of the slice of bread with a generous drizzle of good quality olive oil and a pinch of salt. On a hot grill or griddle, grill each side for about 4–5 minutes until crisp. Any leftover grilled bread can be used up and blitzed into breadcrumbs or croutons for a soup or salad the next day.

A fun idea for a large dinner party is to have a large board or platter with separate topping options in various bowls alongside grilled bread so people can help themselves. If you do this, cut them into smaller, bite-size pieces so your guests will still have hearty appetites! It's easy to fill up on bruschetta, so be mindful. Serve the bruschetta on a large wooden board or tray with a nice glass of wine.

HEIRLOOM TOMATOES WITH BASIL & BUFFALO MOZZARELLA

Serves 6

3–4 large heirloom tomatoes of any
    variety
Extra-virgin olive oil
4–6 oz fresh buffalo mozzarella
A bunch of fresh basil
Quality aged balsamic vinegar
Maldon salt
Fresh cracked black pepper

Slice the tomatoes into thin rounds, about ¼" thick. They may be irregular in shape but that's okay, as long as they are ripe.

Take one large ball of mozzarella and slice it evenly into thin rounds. Slice as many balls as needed.

To assemble the bruschetta, layer together the tomatoes and mozzarella with a fresh basil leaf on the grilled bread.

Drizzle a splash of balsamic vinegar and a good drizzle of olive oil, using your thumb on top of the bottle to control the flow. Sprinkle with Maldon salt and a few cracks of fresh ground black pepper.

ROASTED CHERRIES WITH GORGONZOLA, HONEY, & THYME

Serves 6

1 lb (500 g) Bing or rainier cherries,
    pitted and halved
Extra-virgin olive oil
Kosher salt
½ lb (230 g) gorgonzola wedge
Wildflower honey
Fresh thyme leaves
Maldon salt

Preheat the oven to 400°F and prepare a small roasting pan lined with aluminum foil.

Place the pitted cherries in the roasting pan. Drizzle the cherries lightly with olive oil and a pinch of kosher salt.

Roast the cherries for 15–20 minutes, turning once with a wooden spoon until the cherries are soft, juicy, and caramelized.

Let the cherries slightly cool before assembling; they can be quite hot and sticky!

To assemble one bruschetta, slice a thick chunk of gorgonzola and smear it gently onto the toasted bread. Spoon the roasted cherries over the cheese. Drizzle a bit of honey on top, a sprinkle of thyme leaves, and finish with a pinch of Maldon salt.

SUMMER GARDEN CAPONATA

Serves 8

2 eggplants (1.5–2 lb), diced into
    small ½" cubes

Kosher salt

Extra-virgin olive oil

1 red bell pepper, diced

1 red onion, thinly sliced

1 medium zucchini, diced

1 medium yellow squash, diced

2 garlic cloves, minced

4 (1 lb or 500 g) medium tomatoes
    (whatever is fresh to you), diced

1 cup (180 g) Castelvetrano olives,
    pitted

2 tablespoons caper berries

¼ cup (300 ml) dry white wine

Handful fresh basil, roughly torn

Handful fresh mint, roughly torn

Preheat the oven to 400°F. Line a roasting pan with aluminum foil.

Place the eggplant cubes into a large bowl. Sprinkle a handful of salt over the eggplant, and using your hands or a wooden spoon, evenly coat all the pieces. Let them sit for 20 minutes to remove some of the bitterness.

While the eggplant is resting, gather a large sauté pan or Dutch oven. Add a generous 4 or 5 tablespoons of olive oil to the pan over medium-low heat.

Add the red pepper, red onions, zucchini, squash, and garlic to the pan.

Let the vegetables cook for 10–12 minutes, stirring occasionally as they wilt down.

While the vegetables are cooking, lightly rinse the eggplant in a colander to wash off some of the excess salt. Place the eggplant on the roasting pan with a generous drizzle of olive oil over the pieces.

Roast the eggplant for 20–25 minutes, turning once or twice, until soft and golden.

While the eggplant is roasting, continue cooking the remaining vegetables by adding the tomatoes, olives, and capers. Reduce the heat to low and combine everything together and continue to cook until it is gently broken down and soft.

Once the eggplant is finished, add it to the remaining vegetables.

Pour in the white wine, gently stirring it in until thoroughly combined. Let the caponata simmer for 5 minutes.

Season with kosher salt and cracked black pepper to taste.

Lightly sprinkle in the fresh basil and mint.

Serve warm or at room temperature on a freshly grilled slice of bread with fresh ricotta.

Garnish with sprigs of basil or mint.

BAKED FETA WITH OLIVES & CHERRY TOMATOES

Serves 6–8

2 teaspoons fresh thyme leaves

1 teaspoon fresh rosemary, minced

Dash of red pepper flakes

2 teaspoons fresh oregano, minced

1 tablespoon Italian pine nuts, minced

1¼ cups (about 160 g) whole
  Kalamata olives

Extra-virgin olive oil

8 oz (227 g) traditional block feta
  in brine

1 cup (about 135 g) whole
  Castelvetrano olives

1 tablespoon caper berries

3 whole garlic cloves

1 cup (roughly 150 g) whole cherry
  tomatoes

½ lemon, cut into thin slices

Kosher salt to taste

Cracked black pepper

This dish is a love note to the Greek isles with briny feta, olives, and good quality olive oil. Despite looking somewhat like a slapdash sort of dish, this starter is one of my favorites to slather on crusty bread with a crisp Assyrtiko or Sauvignon Blanc in the sun. It's merely a matter of assembly of high-quality ingredients that are reminiscent of a blissful Aegean holiday.

Preheat the oven to 350°F and gather a 9" rimmed baking or casserole dish.

Roughly chop a quarter of the Kalamata olives for the tapenade, removing the pits. The remaining whole olives will be added later.

In a small mixing bowl, combine the thyme, rosemary, red pepper flakes, oregano, pine nuts, chopped Kalamata olives, and a tablespoon of olive oil until evenly distributed like a spread.

Place the block of feta into the center of the baking dish.

Spoon the tapenade over the top of the feta, covering it completely.

Scatter the remaining whole Kalamata and Castelvetrano olives, caper berries, garlic cloves, and cherry tomatoes around the feta. (Remind your guests later of the pits!)

Top the feta block with a lemon slice and add the remaining slices around the dish.

Add a good drizzle of olive oil over the dish with a pinch of kosher salt and cracked black pepper.

Bake for 25–30 minutes, gently turning the olive and tomatoes once, until the feta is soft and the tomatoes have slightly popped and are juicy.

You can place the dish under the broiler for a few minutes for extra color.

Garnish with fresh thyme or oregano sprigs and serve immediately with fresh garlic crostini.

Garlic Crostini

1 artisan country loaf, ciabatta, or baguette, sliced

4 tablespoons extra-virgin olive oil

1 garlic clove, minced

1 teaspoon kosher salt

Preheat the grill on high or turn on the broiler.

In a small bowl, combine the olive oil, garlic, and salt.

Brush each slice of bread with a spoonful of the garlic oil on each side.

Place the slices on the grill under the broiler and toast until slightly charred and crisp, about 2 minutes on each side. (I like to get the grill marks.)

Serve warm on a cutting board alongside the baked feta.

GRILLED OYSTERS WITH HERB & LEMON BUTTER

Serves 4-6

8–12 oysters (at least 2 per person)

12 tablespoons (2 sticks) high quality
    salted butter, room temperature

3 tablespoons fresh chives, minced

2 tablespoons flat-leaf parsley, minced

1 tablespoon oregano, minced

1 tablespoon tarragon, minced

1 tablespoon fresh thyme leaves

Zest of one lemon

Dash of hot sauce or a pinch of red
    pepper flakes

Lemon wedges to serve

Fresh oysters are a real treat; they feel luxurious and indulgent. With their briny juice that sings of the sea, they are like a divine drop of the big blue. Grilling oysters couldn't be easier; there is no shucking required. The tinge of smoke paired with melted butter adds depth to these succulent jewels of the ocean. They are a chic yet easy appetizer for a summer soirée. Try pairing them with a Fino sherry, muscadet, or the beloved bubbly that is champagne.

In a stand mixer with a paddle attachment, combine the butter, chives, parsley, oregano, tarragon, thyme, and lemon zest. Whip the butter on high for about 2–3 minutes until creamy and smooth.

Scrape out the butter and add it to a small serving bowl. Chill the butter in the fridge for at least 30 minutes until firm.

Wash and scrub the oysters well, removing any grit and sea residue. No need to shuck them as they will pop right open due to the heat. Discard any oyster that is already opened.

When you are ready to serve, fire up the grill on high heat. Once it's nice and hot (using smoldering coals or gas), place the hump side of the oyster with the flat side up onto the grill.

Grill the oysters for about 3–5 minutes until the juices begin to run and steam out. They will begin to pop open slightly, even if it's a mere crack. Carefully remove them from the grill with tongs and discard any unopened oysters (or give them another minute or two to see if they eventually open). Using an oven mitt and a small knife, cut the oyster away from the top shell and continue to gently pry open the oyster. Try and preserve the succulent juices inside as you crack them open. Toss the top shell away and add a small dollop of herb butter to each oyster.

Serve the oysters immediately or over ice and offer your guests optional hot sauce, red pepper flakes, or an additional squeeze of lemon.

CASTELVETRANO
OLIVE BREADSTICKS

Makes 14 breadsticks

2¼ teaspoons (7 g) active dry yeast

1½ cups (358 ml) lukewarm water

3½ cups (440 g) bread flour

4 tablespoons extra-virgin olive oil

1½ (10 grams) teaspoons kosher salt

1 5.3-oz jar (150 g) pitted
  Castelvetrano olives in brine,
  drained and roughly chopped

A pile of warm and soft breadsticks is a welcoming sight indeed. Dipped in the garlicky herb oil, they are rather addicting! My family eats bread ravenously, and whether it's a rustic loaf or these breadsticks straight from the oven, there is always a fresh loaf on our outdoor table. Bread is communal and convivial, meant to be torn and shared.

In a stand mixer with an attached dough hook or large bowl, combine the yeast and half of the water. Stir together until the yeast is dissolved. Let it stand for 10 minutes until slightly bubbly and frothy. If the mix shows no sign of activity, the yeast may be old. Repeat the step with fresh yeast.

Add the flour to the bowl and begin to knead the dough on a slow speed while gradually adding the remaining water and olive oil in a slow and steady stream.

Scrape the sides of the bowl if necessary and add the salt and continue to knead the dough for 1–2 minutes until it just comes together.

Let the dough rest for another 15 minutes.

Add the olives and continue to knead the dough on medium speed for 5 minutes until the dough is soft, springy, and the olives are well incorporated.

Let the dough rise, covered with a tea towel in a warm spot, for at least one hour until puffy. While the dough rises, preheat the oven to 425°F and prepare a parchment-lined baking sheet.

Once the dough is puffy and doubled in size, pour out the dough onto a lightly dusted work surface.

Slightly pat down the dough into a rough log. Using a bench scraper, divide the dough crosswise into roughly 14 equal portions. You can further divide these again to double the number of breadsticks.

Begin to shape each breadstick by taking one portion onto the lightly dusted flour surface. Using the palms of your hands, starting from the center, roll the dough away to the outside to form a long log, about 10–12" long. You may need to keep rolling starting from the middle working outward to create an evenly thick breadstick. Place the breadstick onto the parchment paper.

Continue to shape each portion of dough, lining them up on the baking sheet with ½"–1" space between each.

Bake the breadsticks for 15 minutes until they are a light golden brown. They should be soft and tender.

If the breadsticks are baked together, gently tear them apart individually.

Serve them warm with the fresh herb olive oil dip.

Fresh Herb Olive Oil Dip

1 cup (250 ml) extra-virgin olive oil
1 teaspoon fresh oregano, roughly chopped
1 teaspoon fresh rosemary, minced
½ teaspoon fresh thyme leaves
2 garlic cloves, minced
½ teaspoon kosher salt
Dash of red pepper flakes

In a small serving bowl, stir all the ingredients together until thoroughly combined. To serve, use a small teaspoon for guests to help themselves. (If you have any dip leftover, you can reuse it for a salad vinaigrette or on the grill.)

OFF-THE-VINE GAZPACHO

Serves 6

1 lb (about 2 large ones) heirloom
  tomatoes, cored and cut into chunks
1 lb (about 5) Roma tomatoes, cored
  and cut into chunks
1 small cucumber, peeled, de-seeded,
  and cut into chunks
1 medium red bell pepper, cored and
  sliced into thick strips
¼ red onion, cut into large pieces
2 garlic cloves
Extra-virgin olive oil
1 teaspoon kosher salt
2 tablespoons red wine vinegar
1 tablespoon coriander
½ teaspoon ground cumin
Fresh cracked black pepper

Simple Herb Croutons:
3–4 slices sourdough or quality day-
  old bread, cut into small chunks
  about ½"–¼"
½ teaspoon minced rosemary
½ teaspoon dried oregano
½ teaspoon kosher salt
Extra-virgin olive oil

I love to make fresh gazpacho for a hot August get-together. It's refreshing and healthy. Using a variety of the plumpest tomatoes you can get your hands on sets it apart with a sultry depth of flavor. You will want to be sipping on this all season long.

In a food processor or blender, add the tomatoes, cucumber, red pepper, red onion, garlic, and 3 tablespoons of olive oil. You can also work in batches if needed.

Blend for a minute or two until smooth (depending on your consistency preference, I like mine on the smoother side).

Add the salt, red wine vinegar, coriander, and cumin and pulse several times.

Pour the gazpacho into a large pitcher and set it in the fridge for at least 3 hours until chilled.

When you are ready to serve, pour the chilled gazpacho into small glasses or bowls and top with the herb croutons and your favorite fresh herbs such as oregano, basil, or parsley. I like to add a nice drizzle of olive oil to each serving to finish it off.

You can also serve the gazpacho in one large pitcher and let your guests help themselves (use small glasses in this case); they can add croutons and choose from a variety of fresh minced herbs in little bowls.

Simple Herb Croutons

Preheat the oven to 350°F and gather a small baking sheet lined with parchment paper or foil.

In a medium-sized mixing bowl, combine the bread, rosemary, oregano, and salt. Drizzle over a few tablespoons of olive oil until the bread is lightly but evenly coated.

Toss the bread together and lay evenly on the baking sheet.

Bake for 12–15 minutes, turning them once or twice, until lightly brown and crisp.

BAKED CAMEMBERT IN A SOURDOUGH BOULE

Serves 6–8

1 round country sourdough boule

1 8-oz (227 g) camembert wheel

3 tablespoons fig jam

1 rosemary sprig

1 teaspoon fresh thyme leaves

1 tablespoon chopped walnuts

2–3 thyme sprigs

Kosher salt

Baked camembert may be a blast from the past, but it is worth keeping around. When a golden summer season sadly draws to a close, this is a tempting starter to welcome autumn. It may have minimal ingredients, but try to source the best ones you can find, especially for the camembert and sourdough boule. It is a standout presentation with the gooey, melted cheese encased in a rustic loaf that guests can't wait to tuck into.

Preheat the oven to 350°F.

To cut out the circle in the boule, place the camembert wheel on top of the loaf and, using a sharp serrated knife, cut into the bread along the edge of the cheese. Continue to slice along the edge, cutting 2"–3" deep and remove the soft center and top. Gently nestle the wheel into the hole and cut away any extra bits of bread, so the cheese can fit in snuggly.

Lightly score the top of the camembert with an X.

Spoon the fig jam evenly on top of the camembert. Tear off a bit of the rosemary and tuck it on top of the cheese. Sprinkle with thyme, chopped walnuts, and a pinch of kosher salt.

Line a baking sheet with aluminum foil and bake for 15 minutes until the cheese is gooey and soft.

Garnish with fresh thyme sprigs and serve warm with additional baguette slices or crackers. And, of course, slice up the loaf once you're finished!

SALADS & SIDES

It wouldn't be a summer gathering without a vibrant and crunchy salad. Nearly anything can be tossed in—nuts, dried fruit, or the best of the summer's lush produce. I love to include something green and fresh on my table. I simply can't get enough dark leafy greens and summer veggies. A table spread of big bowls of garden greens, grilled veggie platters, and heaping piles of grains is my kind of summer meal. The salads and sides you'll find in this section are inexpensive yet substantial. Rather than centering a meal on a meat dish, I often prefer a mish-mash of many sides and a big seasonal salad. They are great for potlucks that can add delicious variety to the table. These recipes are honest and simple, giving the seasonal harvest center stage. Our summers on the farm were spent picking and plucking the beets and kale and finding the hidden cauliflower under the leaves. It brings such joy to see hard labor reap such beautiful and delicious rewards. Summer's heirloom tomatoes are the star in the caprese recipes on page 85-86. These recipes are meant to be effortless and intuitive for any outdoor gathering. Centering a meal on the garden or what you've picked up at the farmers market is a healthy and happy way to entertain, and dare I say, live!

A BUTTERY GREEN SALAD

Serves 6

2 heads butter lettuce

1 large watermelon radish, thinly sliced into half-moons[1]

1 large handful snow peas, cut on the diagonal into ½" spears

2 baby English cucumbers, thinly sliced into rounds

½ cup (117 g) chopped walnuts

1 ripe avocado, sliced into crescent moons

Optional: Simple Herb Croutons (page 68)

For the dressing:

¼ cup (59 ml) buttermilk

3 tablespoons sour cream

3 tablespoons extra-virgin olive oil–based mayonnaise

2 tablespoon fresh chives, minced (reserve one to garnish)

1 tablespoon flat-leaf parsley, minced

1 tablespoon fresh dill, minced

1 garlic clove, minced

½ teaspoon whole grain mustard

Juice ½ lemon

¼ teaspoon kosher salt

Every home cook needs a good green salad in their recipe book. This buttery salad is one to include with its snappy snow peas and creamy buttermilk dressing. I also love the beautiful pattern the butter lettuce creates, like a budding rose. Texture is a key ingredient for any salad, and this salad ticks all the boxes. It is a step-up, and an easy one at that, from a basic green salad, and it's an excellent choice for any low-key outdoor gathering.

Gently tear off the butter lettuce leaves from the core, leaving them whole. Give them a thorough rinse and pat them dry with a paper towel.

In a large shallow serving bowl, arrange the lettuce leaves in a flower blossom–type pattern, similar to its original shape.

Sprinkle on the radish slices, snow peas, cucumbers, and walnuts. Add avocado slices on top.

Spoon the dressing over the salad if you are serving immediately, or serve it in a small pitcher on the side for your guests to pour on when it's time to eat.

Sprinkle over the reserved tablespoon of minced chives after you dress the salad.

This is the only salad that I prefer not to immediately toss, as I like to retain the lovely blossom look of the lettuce.

Dressing

Whisk together all the ingredients in a small bowl and transfer to a small pitcher. Give it a taste and season accordingly if needed. I would make two batches of the dressing in case there is a greedy one in the bunch!

» 1   *Use a mandolin slicer if you have one.*

HERB POTATO SALAD WITH GREEN BEANS & LEMON

Serves 6

3 lb (1.3 kg) mixed potatoes such as
    red, purple, and yellow, cut into
    quarters roughly the same size
1 generous handful (about 220g)
    yellow and/or green string beans,
    ends trimmed and cut into ½" pieces
1 small red onion, thinly sliced
1 large red radish, thinly sliced
1 handful flat-leaf parsley,
    roughly chopped
3 tablespoons minced garlic chives
3 tablespoons dill, roughly chopped
2 tablespoons fresh oregano,
    roughly chopped

For the lemon vinaigrette:
Juice of 2 lemons
1 heaping tablespoon whole
    ground mustard
1 garlic clove, minced
1 tablespoon white wine vinegar
1 teaspoon kosher salt
Fresh cracked black pepper
½ cup (118 ml) extra-virgin olive oil

A good potato salad is an American picnic classic. Every grandmother has a famous recipe that is always requested at family summer gatherings. This version is a lighter and crunchier option with fresh green beans, handfuls of herbs, and lots of lemon. A tricolor potato mix makes it a vibrant presentation for such a straightforward salad. The fresh herbs in this recipe are treated like a star ingredient just as much as the colorful potatoes.

Place the potatoes in a large stockpot over high heat and fill with water, covering them by 3 inches.

Cook the potatoes for about 10–12 minutes until slightly tender. The water may slightly be boiling at this point.

Once the water is just about boiling, add the green beans to the pot. Continue to cook until the green beans and potatoes are tender, about another 12 minutes. The beans should be firm but not too snappy or too soft. If you pierce the potatoes with a knife, it should slide through easily.

Drain the green beans and potatoes and run them under cold water. Set aside them to cool, although they don't need to be completely cold.

Prepare the vinaigrette by combining the lemon juice, ground mustard, garlic, white wine vinegar, salt, and a few cracks of black pepper in a mason jar or small bowl. Pour in the olive oil while continuously whisking until the vinaigrette is smooth and emulsified.

Gather a large mixing bowl and combine the potatoes, green beans, red onion slices, radish slices, parsley, garlic chives, dill, and oregano.

Pour the vinaigrette over the salad and gently toss it together until everything is evenly coated.

Garnish with a few sprigs of dill, parsley, or radish slices and serve immediately or cold. This salad also is delicious when made ahead; just give it a good toss with some fresh olive oil.

BURRATA WITH MELON & PROSCIUTTO

Serves 4–6

½ lb (226 g) fresh burrata

½ medium cantaloupe, sliced into crescents

4 oz (about 10–12 slices) quality aged prosciutto di Parma

2 ripe heirloom tomatoes, thinly sliced into rounds

A few fresh figs halved or peach slices

Handful fresh basil, roughly torn

Extra-virgin olive oil

Quality aged balsamic vinegar

Maldon or other coarse sea salt

Cracked black pepper

The traditional summertime duo gets an update with luscious burrata and fresh figs. No wonder the Italians love these two married together—it's a sultry pairing for a balmy summer evening. Try and source the best ingredients you can find; it is only worth serving if they are top-notch. Trust the Italians when it comes to entertaining al fresco; they know how to do it right!

First, assemble this salad moments before you sit down; it's best served fresh.

To assemble the salad, place the burrata rounds on the platter, either one in the center or scattered around the platter, depending on how many rounds you have.

Using your hands, wrap the center of each wedge of melon with a strip of the prosciutto.

Alternate layering the tomato slices and prosciutto-wrapped cantaloupe slices around the burrata on the plate.

Tuck in the figs or peach slices in the remaining gaps.

Sprinkle fresh basil over the top.

Add a good amount of olive oil and a splattering of balsamic vinegar.

Season with a pinch of Maldon salt and cracked black pepper, and serve immediately.

STONE FRUIT PANZANELLA

Serves 6

4–5 slices day-old bread, either sourdough or an artisanal country-style boule

2 lbs (roughly 700g) variety (5–6) of stone fruit such as peaches, nectarines, plums, apricots, pitted and thinly sliced

½ head of radicchio, roughly chopped

1 large heirloom tomato, thinly sliced, or 1 large handful cherry tomatoes, halved

1 large handful arugula, roughly torn

1 handful basil, roughly torn

5–6 ripe figs, halved

½ cup (150 g) ricotta salata, roughly crumbled

Extra-virgin olive oil

Quality aged balsamic vinegar

Kosher salt

Cracked black pepper

The beauty of Panzanella is that it transforms a dull—even stale—bread into something new and wonderful. It is an ideal foundation for tossing in what's readily available or what's ripe and in season. Ambrosial stone fruits are heavenly additions that liven up this crisp salad. Grilling the bread beforehand adds a smoky component. I also find that, when prepped this way, it holds up better over time, especially in the heat of a lazy weekend lunch.

Preheat the grill to high heat.

Set the bread slices face-up on a cutting board and drizzle each side with good olive oil. (You can also use a pastry brush.) Season each oiled side with a pinch of kosher salt.

Once the grates are nice and hot, place each slice of bread on the grill and toast each side for 3–5 minutes until you get lovely crisp grill marks on both sides. Remove them from the grill once they are toasty and golden; they burn easily, so don't step away from the grill!

Once the bread has slightly cooled, roughly tear the slices into small chunks about 1"–2" wide. I prefer the rustic and authentic torn look for this salad instead of cutting them with a knife.

In a large serving bowl, combine the sliced stone fruit, radicchio, tomatoes, arugula, basil, figs, and the grilled bread chunks.

Drizzle a good glug of olive oil and a few splashes of balsamic vinegar over the salad. Season with a pinch of salt and gently toss everything together.

Sprinkle on the crumbled ricotta salata and season with a few cracks of black pepper.

Serve immediately with a crisp glass of sauvignon blanc or a dry prosecco!

CUCUMBER & ORANGE WATERCRESS SALAD WITH CARAWAY

Serves 4–6

1 medium garden or English cucumber, about 1 lb

¼ cup (18 g) sliced almonds

5 oz watercress (about 4 big handfuls), stalky ends trimmed

1 large navel orange, peeled with pith removed and sliced into wedges

¼ cup (200 g) crumbled feta

1 handful fresh mint, roughly torn

Optional: 1 handful micro arugula

For the vinaigrette:

Juice ½ navel orange (about 50 ml)

1 heaping tablespoon orange zest

3 tablespoons white wine vinegar

½ teaspoon wildflower honey

1 heaping tablespoon caraway seeds

½ teaspoon kosher salt

Fresh cracked black pepper

¼ cup (59 ml) extra-virgin olive oil

This salad is a refreshing and light alternative to a basic green salad on a hot summer day. Crisp and cool cucumbers are one of the season's most abundant veggies too. On a lazy July afternoon, when I'm not in the mood for cooking, I love to slice them up and toss them with invigorating herbs like mint. The caraway seeds and almonds add a satisfying crunch to the ever-plentiful summer cucumber. This is a great salad to double servings for a large party.

Everyone has their preference for peeling cucumbers; I like to leave a little bit of the crunchy green skin. In general, if the skin is smooth and not too waxy, I peel only 4 sides of the cucumber, like stripes. You can, of course, peel and remove the seeds if you wish. Whichever way you choose, slice the cucumber into ¼" rounds.

In a small skillet, add the slivered almonds over medium heat. Lightly toast the almonds for 2 or 3 minutes, stirring until fragrant. Keep an eye on these; they can burn quickly.

Prepare the vinaigrette by gathering a small mixing bowl or mason jar. Squeeze in the orange juice and add the orange zest, white wine vinegar, honey, caraway seeds, and kosher salt to the jar. Season with a few cracks of black pepper.

Gradually pour in the olive oil as you simultaneously whisk the vinaigrette until it becomes emulsified and smooth.

Gather your serving bowl and add the watercress, cucumbers, and oranges. Drizzle over the vinaigrette and lightly toss the salad together.

Sprinkle the toasted sliced almonds, crumbled feta, mint, and the micro arugula on top of the salad and serve immediately.

A BETTER CAPRESE

Serves 4–6

5–6 variety of heirloom tomatoes
 such as Brandywine, Evergreen, or
 Cherokee purple, thinly sliced into
 rounds

Kosher salt

1 tablespoon caper berries

½ cup (90 g) assorted olives such as
 Kalamata, Castelvetrano, Niçoise,
 pitted and halved

8 oz (227 g) fresh buffalo mozzarella
 (burrata works equally well)

1 generous handful fresh basil

Quality aged balsamic vinegar

Extra-virgin olive oil

The tried-and-true caprese salad may be a common recipe for the outdoor table, but this salad has a place in my heart. Every summer on the farm, our garden is overloaded with tantalizing tomatoes of all shapes, colors, and varieties. August dinners on the porch usually consist of fresh slices of garden tomatoes, luscious mozzarella, torn basil plucked a few moments prior, good olive oil, and a healthy sprinkling of sea salt. This dish epitomizes summer on the farm for me, and this recipe adds a few briny accompaniments. This salad never gets old!

On a large platter, layer the tomato slices alternating in color and size.

Generously season the tomatoes with a good pinch or two of salt and let them sit for at least 15 minutes. A good tomato comes to life when sprinkled with salt and left to rest.

Sprinkle on the capers and olives.

If you have a whole mozzarella ball, gently tear it and scatter it over the tomatoes. If they are individual, you can either tear them in half or nestle them in whole. Add another tiny pinch of salt to the dish.

Gently tear the basil leaves with your hands and sprinkle them haphazardly over the top.

Add a splash of balsamic vinegar and a liberal drizzle of olive oil over the entire platter.

Serve immediately with good, crusty bread to soak up the sweet juices.

A DIFFERENT CAPRESE

Serves 4–6

4–6 heirloom tomatoes, sliced into
¼" rounds (aim for one tomato
per person)
2 generous handfuls cherry tomatoes
8 oz (227 g) fresh buffalo mozzarella
Quality aged balsamic vinegar
Extra-virgin olive oil
1 handful basil, roughly torn
Maldon salt or other flaky sea salt
Fresh cracked black pepper

I adore this salad so much that I had to include two variations. A traditional caprese, using the best ingredients, of course, is always fresh. This recipe, however, adds a bit of char and smoke to the dish by lightly grilling the tomato slices. As a result, the tomatoes will be softer, which creates a sweet juice for mopping up with some good bread. The key is having the grill piping hot before placing the oiled tomatoes on the grates. It only takes a minute or so on the grill, but I find it adds depth and dimension to the overall salad.

Since this takes just moments to assemble, I like to start grilling once everyone is settled, chatting away, and ready to eat. It's best served while still warm, fresh off the grill.

Preheat the grill to high heat. Be sure to scrape the grill clean or else any old bits may stick to the tomatoes.

On a large platter, drizzle the tomato slices with olive oil evenly on both sides. In a small bowl, add the cherry tomatoes and again lightly drizzle them with olive oil.

Once the grill is nice and hot, at least 450°F, place the tomato rounds on the grill. Using a grill basket, place the cherry tomatoes inside and set it on top of the grill. (If you don't have a grill basket, you can use skewers; just be sure to soak the wood ones in water beforehand.)

Grill the tomato slices for 2 minutes until slightly charred and gently flip them with a large spatula and continue to grill the other side of the tomato for another 2 minutes. Then take them off the grill once they begin to char. Try not to touch or move them too much, so they retain distinct grill marks.

Toss or stir the cherry tomatoes in the basket until they become slightly blistered, about 5 minutes, and then remove them from the grill. (Follow this same step if using skewers.)

Gather your serving platter and layer the tomatoes on the plate. They will be juicer and softer, so handle them with care.

Scatter the grilled cherry tomatoes over the other rounds.

Using your hands, tear the mozzarella into bite-size pieces and scatter them over the platter. Drizzle a tablespoon or so of balsamic vinegar and olive oil over the tomatoes and mozzarella.

Sprinkle the torn basil over the platter. Season with a few pinches of Maldon salt and fresh cracked black pepper.

TROPICS SLAW

Serves 6

1 lb head red cabbage (small)

1 lb head green cabbage (small)

2 medium carrots, grated

1 red onion, thinly sliced

2 ripe mangos, either diced into ½"
    cubes or sliced into small wedges

1 generous handful of cilantro,
    roughly chopped

3 large limes

1 heaping tablespoon lime zest

1½ teaspoons kosher salt

¼ teaspoon fresh cracked
    black pepper

½ cup (118 ml) extra-virgin olive oil

This crunchy and rainbow-hued slaw is a great addition to the outdoor table, especially with the Maui Mahi Mahi Burgers on page 117. When I first tasted a Maui mango, I nearly gasped because of how juicy and flavorful they were compared to the mealy and bland ones I had on the mainland. Truly a fruit of the gods! If you can't get your hands on a good mango, a ripe pineapple is equally delicious. Rather than a heavier mayo-based slaw, this is a fresh side dish that naturally rounds out a summer picnic or barbecue with a hint of the tropics.

Cut both cabbages into quarters, removing the tough core at the bottom. With the flat face of the cabbage placed on the cutting board, finely shred the cabbages as thin as possible.

Combine shredded cabbages, carrots, red onion, mango, and cilantro in a large bowl.

For the dressing, squeeze the limes into a small bowl and add the lime zest, salt, and a few cracks of black pepper. Drizzle in the olive oil while simultaneously whisking until smooth.

Pour the dressing over the slaw and gently toss it together and add more olive oil if needed.

Serve a scoop of slaw in the Maui Mahi Mahi Burger (page 117) or on the side.

VERMONT BACKROAD BAKED BEANS

Serves 4–6

1 lb (454 g) dry navy or great
    northern beans, rinsed and
    drained*

½ teaspoon baking soda

1 yellow onion, diced

2 garlic cloves, minced

2 bay leaves (fresh if you can find
    them)

6 strips uncured maple smoked
    bacon; you can also use hickory or
    applewood smoked, diced

¾ cup (177 ml) pure Vermont maple
    syrup Grade B

½ cup (118 ml) dark unsulphured
    molasses

¼ cup (55 g) dark brown sugar

½ tablespoon whole grain mustard

1 scant tablespoon apple cider
    vinegar

1 teaspoon kosher salt

* ¼ cup reserved bean cooking water

A proper potluck isn't complete without baked beans. They are an ode to my love of all things maple. They are a classic partner for just about anything hot off the grill, including the sausages on page 130. These beans are the right medley of sweet and savory meant to be wiped clean off the plate!

The night before your gathering, add the beans to a large bowl, cover them with 6–8 cups (about 1500 ml) of water and baking soda, and soak them overnight.

For a quick soak, add the beans and baking soda to a large stockpot and cover them with water by 2". Bring the beans to a soft boil for 15 minutes and then turn off the heat and let them sit for 1 hour. Drain and rinse the beans and continue to follow the steps below.

After the overnight soak, add the beans to a large stockpot or Dutch oven and cover with water by 2". Add the onion, garlic, and bay leaves and bring the beans to a low boil for 2–3 minutes. Lower the heat to a simmer and continue to cook the beans for at least 1 hour until the beans are soft and tender.

Once the beans are tender, drain them, remove the bay leaves, and reserve 1 cup of the cooking water for later use. Set the beans aside while you prepare the following ingredients.

Preheat the oven to 350°F.

Add the diced bacon to a large Dutch oven over medium heat and cook the bacon for 3–5 minutes until it's slightly crisp and the fat is fully rendered. At this point you can either remove the bacon, blot it, drain out the fat, and return the bacon to the pan or simply leave it all in. I prefer to leave a little fat in the pan because it adds flavor.

Add the beans, maple syrup, dark brown sugar, mustard, apple cider vinegar, and salt to the Dutch oven and bake the beans for about 35–45 minutes until they are soft and rich brown in color. If they dry out, add in the reserved cooking water and season with additional maple syrup or salt.

Serve warm, and if you need to reheat them the following day, simply add a bit of the reserved water to reconstitute them.

GRILLED ROMAINE & RADICCHIO SALAD

Serves 6

2 heads romaine lettuce, washed
    and dried with ends trimmed
1 head radicchio, washed and
    quartered with core removed
Extra-virgin olive oil
3–4 peaches, halved with pit removed
Kosher salt
½ cup (about 112 g)
    gorgonzola crumbles
Optional: pickled red onions

When it comes to grilling, don't be shy about experimenting with your garden greens. Romaine and radicchio work beautifully on the grill since they are compact and robust. The slight char adds a delicious depth to this rather light salad. Since they are halved and quartered, there is less chopping involved, and their lovely intricate layers are on display. It is best grilled when it's just about time to eat so it remains crisp and fresh. It only takes a matter of minutes to dress.

Preheat the grill to medium-high. If using a charcoal grill, be sure that the coals are hot and smoldering.

Cut the heads of romaine lettuce in half lengthwise and split them open in two.

Place the halved romaine, radicchio, and peaches on a large baking tray so that they are open faced.

Drizzle a glug or two of olive oil over the greens and peaches to coat them evenly. Sprinkle with a pinch of kosher salt.

Using tongs, place the romaine, radicchio, and peaches cut-side down on the grill.

Grill the romaine and radicchio for about 3–5 minutes on one side and then turn them only once until the leaves are lightly charred. Flip the peaches to the soft skin side when they have nice grill marks on the cut face. Try not to step away from the grill as the greens crisp up in a matter of minutes. Otherwise, they will turn soggy and wilt.

Once the greens and peaches have a good char on every side, remove them from the grill and place them back onto the same tray. Let them cool while you prepare the croutons and dressing.

To assemble the salad, alternate laying the romaine and radicchio on the platter. Nestle in the grilled peaches and sprinkle on the croutons, gorgonzola crumbles, and pickled red onions. Drizzle over the dressing if you are serving it immediately, otherwise use a small bowl for guests to help themselves. The dressing on the side keeps the salad crisp and fresh throughout the meal.

Herb & Garlic Croutons

3 cups (200 g or 0.5 lb) stale sourdough or ciabatta, cubed into ½"–1" pieces
Extra-virgin olive oil
1 tablespoon herbs de Provence
2 garlic cloves, minced
½ teaspoon kosher salt

Preheat the oven to 350°F. Prepare a parchment-lined 9" x 13" baking sheet.

Add the bread pieces to a large mixing bowl.

Drizzle enough olive oil to lightly coat the bread pieces, tossing them with a spoon or your hands.

Sprinkle on the herbs de Provence, garlic cloves, and kosher salt. Combine the bread and herbs until everything is well coated.

Spread the bread pieces evenly onto the baking sheet.

Bake for 25 minutes, turning once or twice with a wood spatula until crisp.

Let them cool slightly before sprinkling over the salad.

Gorgonzola & Greek Yogurt Dressing

3 heaping tablespoons plain full-fat Greek yogurt
1–1.5 oz (about 35 grams) gorgonzola wedge
2 tablespoons red wine vinegar
⅔ cup (160 ml) extra-virgin olive oil
Kosher salt to taste
Cracked black pepper

In a food processor or blender, combine the Greek yogurt, gorgonzola, and red wine vinegar. Turn on the blender and simultaneously pour in the olive oil and blend until smooth. Scrape the bottom, if necessary, to incorporate any remaining bits of cheese.

Season with salt and black pepper to taste.

GARDEN GREEN BEANS WITH CHILI & ALMONDS

Serves 4–6

4 tablespoons extra-virgin olive oil

1 large shallot, minced

2 lbs (about 900 g) string green beans, ends trimmed

½ cup (118 ml) water

3 cloves garlic, minced

1½ teaspoons kosher salt

½ lemon

1 tablespoon crushed red pepper flakes

½ cup (46 g) sliced almonds

Cracked black pepper

On our farm, we have a towering windmill in our garden. Every summer, you can barely see the frame behind the twisting and rambling green bean vines that snake up to the tippy top. The snappy green beans hang like dangling earrings hiding behind the leaves, and we pick and pluck them all summer long. This is a stripped-down recipe that celebrates the purity of these snappy green beans. Chili gives them a rather addictive kick!

In a large sauté pan, add the olive oil and shallots over medium-low heat. Sauté for 5–7 minutes until the shallots are soft and translucent.

Add the green beans and ¼ of the water to the pan and give them a quick stir. Cover the pan with a fitted lid and lower the heat.

Cook the green beans, stirring occasionally, until tender and bright in color. Add a few tablespoons of water if it dries out, just enough to gently steam the green beans.

Add the garlic and salt and continue to sauté for another 2–3 minutes. Give a bean a taste—it should be tender but not too crunchy or flimsy.

Squeeze a lemon half over the green beans and turn off the heat.

Transfer the green beans to a serving platter and sprinkle on the red pepper flakes and slivered almonds. Drizzle a little olive oil over the beans and add a few cracks of black pepper.

I prefer to serve them warm, but they are equally delicious cold.

SWEET PEPPER WILD RICE SALAD

Serves 6

2 cups (360 g) wild rice

1 medium yellow bell pepper, diced

1 medium red bell pepper, diced

1 medium green bell pepper, diced

1 medium red onion, diced

3 celery stalks, diced

1 cup (120 g) chopped walnuts

1 cup (150 g) dried cherries,
    unsweetened

1 generous handful (30 g) flat-leaf
    parsley, chopped

2 heaping tablespoons orange zest

½ cup (118 ml) fresh orange juice
    (about 1 orange squeezed)

3 tablespoons champagne vinegar

1 teaspoon kosher salt

1 teaspoon fresh cracked black pepper

¾ cup (177 ml) extra-virgin olive oil

A colorful salad like this one should be on any outdoor table. The orange zest adds a fresh and unexpected zing to the salad. The dried cherries make this salad pop, and if fresh ones are in season, without a doubt, use those little beauties! This is a family favorite for summertime potlucks. It is a light yet substantial dish perfect for serving all summer long.

Cook the rice according to the packet's instructions while preparing the remaining ingredients.

Gather a serving bowl and combine the diced peppers, red onion, celery, walnuts, dried cherries, and parsley.

Once the rice has cooked, fluff it up on a large plate and stick it in the fridge to allow it to cool slightly.

Begin to prepare the vinaigrette in a small bowl or mason jar by adding the orange zest, orange juice, champagne vinegar, salt, and black pepper. Gradually pour in the olive oil as you whisk the vinaigrette until emulsified and smooth. You may want to give it another quick whisk before pouring it over the salad.

Once the rice has cooled, add the rice to your serving bowl with the other ingredients.

Pour in the vinaigrette and toss the salad together. Season with additional salt if necessary. It can be served warm or cold or on a bed of greens.

Garnish with a few sprigs of parsley, dried cherries, and orange zest.

ROASTED BEET & ARUGULA SALAD

Serves 6

6–8 large beets, an assortment of red, golden, and Chioggia, washed, peeled, and cut into 1″ chunks

Extra-virgin olive oil

1 teaspoon kosher salt

Freshly cracked black pepper

3 tablespoons unsalted butter

¼ cup (59 ml) pure Vermont maple syrup

1 cup (125 g) chopped pecans

1 5-oz (142 g) bag baby arugula

½ cup (112 g) Gorgonzola or Stilton cheese, crumbled

1 small handful pea shoots

4–5 thin slices Chioggia beets to garnish

For the dressing:

3 tablespoons pure Vermont maple syrup

2 tablespoons quality aged balsamic vinegar

1 tablespoon stone-ground mustard

½ teaspoon kosher salt

½ cup (118 ml) extra-virgin olive oil

Freshly cracked black pepper to taste

When harvest time arrives on the farm, the beets are one of the most anticipated yields in the lot. Plump ruby and golden ornaments plucked out of the ground have an earthy sweetness. Roasted and piled on peppery arugula with tangy gorgonzola, this is an easy and hearty salad that commemorates the turn of the season with warmth and richness. It is a gorgeously hued salad that gives autumn a happy hello.

Preheat the oven to 450°F and gather a large roasting tray.

Add the diced beets to the roasting tray and drizzle with a liberal amount of olive oil until lightly coated all around. Season with kosher salt and a few cracks of black pepper.

Roast the beets for 45–50 minutes, turning them once or twice until crisp and tender.

While the beets are roasting, prepare the candied pecans by melting the butter in a small skillet over medium-low heat. Add the maple syrup and pecans to the skillet, stirring until the pecans are thoroughly coated. Reduce the heat and continue to stir until the syrup begins to reduce and thicken. Once the nuts are taffy-like, spoon the nuts out onto a piece of parchment paper to cool. Sprinkle over a pinch of salt.

Prepare the dressing by whisking together the maple syrup, balsamic vinegar, mustard, and salt. Whisking continuously, pour in the olive oil and whisk the ingredients together until the oil is emulsified and smooth. Season with a few cracks of black pepper.

Once the beets are slightly cooled, add the baby arugula onto your serving plate. Gently transfer the beets on top of the arugula without tossing the salad.

Add the crumbled gorgonzola, candied pecans, and pea shoots on top of the beets.

Toss the salad together with the dressing once you are ready to serve.

PLATES

When I was a little girl, I watched in curiosity and awe at the feet of my mother in the kitchen as she would whip up the most impressive yet simplest of dishes. She would make roasted garden veggie pasta salad or pillowy burger buns for a feast outside on the terrace. She made it look so easy, multitasking and juggling three or four dishes at a time, not skipping a beat in the conversation. All the while our guests looked on in amazement that matched my own. Perhaps her effortless way of entertaining outside is engrained in me. I enjoy making simple things, both beautiful and delicious as well. Maybe it's a fresh herb salad straight from the garden or farmers market or a sweet blueberry crisp on the menu; the best dishes are made up of the simplest ingredients presented creatively. Letting the main stars of a meal shine is my theory of easy outdoor entertaining. I'm a firm believer that impressive and delicious dishes don't need to be complicated. A true foodie or a culinary novice can appreciate a great outdoor table. Simple, honest, and beautiful home-cooked food shared overlooking the ocean or under the setting summer sun is what it's all about.

Naturally, in the warmer months, we have the urge to call friends around for a barbecue or a low-key dinner party on the terrace. So, with that said, in general, I like to serve light, fresh, and seasonal things, especially since it's this time of the year everything is at its utmost ripest. You'll find that these plates are simple yet exceptional. An easy clam linguine with sweet, sun-kissed cherry tomatoes feels utterly luxurious and special under the summer sun with a crisp glass of pinot grigio (most of the work is scrubbing the clams). A delectable puff pastry tart can look fancy, but it is an effortless dish to throw together for a breezy summer lunch. And, of course, fire up the grill for a juicy strip steak on page 144 with Maui-inspired pineapple salsa for a family barbecue. Being the proud Vermonter that I am, I included a cozy baked sage and butternut lasagna for an autumnal feast on the porch to celebrate the foliage and harvest season. These dishes are meant to take little prep while still special for any outdoor gathering.

Depending on the weather or your mood, choose a plate and mix and match any sides or dessert you like. You will find that most of these recipes can pair easily and complement each other. Or you can choose one main dish and serve a simple, refreshing salad or plate of grilled veggies. Sharing a meal outside should feel and be easy, so relieve yourself of the pressure to create a perfect all-star meal.

GOAT CHEESE & RAINBOW CHARD FRITTATA

Serves 6

3 strips (about 30 g) smoked uncured
    bacon, diced

Extra-virgin olive oil

¾ cup (39 g) red onion, minced
    (reserve a few thin slices or rounds
    to garnish)

1 bunch rainbow chard, stems and
    stalks removed, chopped into ½"
    pieces (about 2 cups cooked)

10 eggs

½ cup (118 ml) half-and-half

½ teaspoon kosher salt

¼ teaspoon cracked black pepper

¼ cup (about 12 g) fresh chives,
    minced (reserve one tablespoon
    wto garnish)

1 cup (150 g) fresh goat cheese

On a lovely June afternoon when the garden begins to bloom, a quick frittata is my trusty standby for an impromptu brunch with friends. It's versatile and can be thrown together in a blink with just a few basic ingredients. Rainbow chard is a robust green that balances the creamy goat cheese nicely. This is a great back-pocket recipe for early summer get-togethers.

Preheat the oven to 400°F. Gather a 9" pre-seasoned cast-iron skillet or a lightly greased 9" x 9" baking tin.

In a 10" sauté pan over medium heat, add the bacon and sauté stirring occasionally until crisp and the fat is fully rendered, about 3 minutes. With a slotted spoon, remove the bacon from the pan onto a paper towel–lined plate. Pat down the excess fat and set aside. Discard the rendered fat in the pan and wipe it clean. In the same pan over low-medium heat, add two tablespoons of olive oil and the red onions. Sauté for about 8–10 minutes until translucent.

Turn the burner down to low and add the Swiss chard to the pan. Sauté for 10 minutes, stirring occasionally until the leaves are lightly wilted. Remove the pan from the heat and season with a pinch of salt and set aside. Continue to prepare the filling by cracking the eggs into a large mixing bowl. Add the half-and-half, salt, cracked black pepper, and chives.

Whisk the egg mixture until smooth and frothy, about a minute or two.

Spread half of the Swiss chard filling evenly into the skillet. With a spoon or your fingers, scatter small crumbles of the goat cheese evenly over the chard filling. Pour in the egg mixture over the filling and cheese. Gently tilt the skillet to ensure that the eggs settle evenly over the filling.

Sprinkle the remaining chard filling over the eggs.

Garnish with a dash of the remaining chives and red onion slices.

Bake the frittata for 8–10 minutes until the eggs are set. Insert a knife in the center to ensure it is cooked through. If the knife comes out clean without any runny eggs, remove the frittata from the oven. If the knife is a little streaky with runny eggs, bake for a few more minutes.

Let the frittata cool slightly before serving straight from the skillet.

PEARL COUSCOUS WITH GRILLED SHRIMP & SUMMER VEGGIES

Serves 6

1 ½ lbs (about 700 g) uncooked wild-caught shrimp, peeled and deveined

For the marinade:

3 tablespoons flat-leaf parsley, minced

1 tablespoon cilantro, minced

1 ½ teaspoons red pepper flakes

3 garlic cloves, minced

¼ teaspoon kosher salt

For the salad:

2 cups (366 g) pearl couscous

3 cups (709 ml) chicken or vegetable stock

Extra-virgin olive oil

Zest of 1 lemon

1 large zucchini, cut into thin strips lengthwise

1 large red onion, quartered

1 lb (about 150 g) cherry tomatoes

1 handful flat-leaf parsley, minced

1 handful cilantro, minced

2 oz (56 g) block feta in brine

Juice of 1 large lemon

The summer garden's bounty is where I constantly turn for recipe inspiration. I find that treating seasonal ingredients, especially summer vegetables, in a straightforward and pure manner is the most wholesome way to share the bounty. Casual summertime gatherings on the farm usually consisted of a large, heaping platter of grilled vegetables plucked straight out of the garden rows. This dish is a slight variation on that summertime staple with garlicky shrimp and savory herb couscous. It's simple but no less delicious and puts the endless supply of summer zucchini to good use!

In a large bowl or Ziploc bag, add the parsley, cilantro, red pepper flakes, garlic, salt, shrimp, and a good drizzle of extra virgin olive oil until every shrimp is evenly coated. Stir or shake until the herbs are distributed throughout.

If you can, it's best to let the shrimp sit overnight in the fridge, but if you're in a pinch, let the shrimp marinate for 3–4 hours in the fridge.

Once you are ready to start cooking, cook the couscous according to the packet's instructions. The stock amount listed above is a general guideline; each brand is slightly different, but I prefer stock over water. Keep the couscous warm and set it aside until ready to serve.

While the couscous is cooking, fire up the grill to high heat and gather a large platter for the veggies.

Place the zucchini strips, tomatoes, and red onion quarters on the platter. Give them a good drizzle of olive oil, lightly coating all sides. Sprinkle on a pinch of kosher salt.

Gather 8–10 metal skewers and add the tomatoes onto as many skewers as needed.

Pull out the shrimp and add them to the skewers. No need to wipe the shrimp clean; just discard the leftover marinade.

Once all your veggies and shrimp are ready to go, set them onto the grill together over high heat.

The cherry tomatoes take the least bit of time to grill, only 4–5 minutes until they start to blister and release their juices, so keep an eye on those.

Remove them immediately once they are done back to a clean platter.

Grill the shrimp until nicely charred and pink, about 5–6 minutes, flipping only once with tongs.

Continue to grill the zucchini for 6–8 minutes, flipping once until tender with nice grill marks on both sides.

Grill the red onion quarters about 5–6 minutes on each side until lightly charred on each side, carefully turning them with tongs to keep them intact.

Once everything is grilled, place everything back onto the platter and gather a large cutting board.

When the zucchini and red onions are cool enough to handle, roughly dice them and add them to a large serving bowl along with the cooked couscous and grilled tomatoes.

Add in the parsley, cilantro, and feta.

Squeeze in the lemon juice and a liberal drizzle of olive oil over the dish. Grate over fresh lemon zest.

Gently toss everything together, taste, and season with additional salt if necessary. Top the salad off with the grilled shrimp and serve warm with additional lemon wedges and cilantro.

COASTAL LINGUINE
WITH CLAMS

Serves 4–6

4 lbs (1.8 kg) cockles or littleneck
    clams
1 lb (484 g) dried or fresh linguine
Extra-virgin olive oil
4 garlic cloves, minced
3 shallots, minced
2 handfuls ripe cherry tomatoes, halved
½ teaspoon red pepper flakes
Kosher salt
½ cup (118 ml) dry white wine
1 handful fresh basil, roughly chopped
1 handful fresh flat-leaf parsley,
    roughly chopped
1 cup (236 ml) reserved pasta water
Fresh cracked black pepper

This dish is the essence of summer for me, with hints of the sea. It conjures memories of the ocean, breathing in the salty air, and basking in the golden sun. As extravagant as the pasta looks with a steaming pile of fresh clams drowned in a garlicky sauce, it is beyond simple and feels celebratory. The sweet juices with a hint of white wine are simply begging to be sopped up with a torn baguette. I love this one for a relaxed yet special occasion.

Add the clams into a large bowl filled with water and gently scrub each one with a scour brush to remove any sandy residue.

In a large sauté pan with a fitted lid, add 4 tablespoons of olive oil over low-medium heat. Add the minced garlic, shallots, halved cherry tomatoes, and red pepper flakes to the pan and sauté for 5 minutes, stirring occasionally, until the garlic and shallots begin to soften.

Bring a large stockpot of liberally salted water to a boil and cook the pasta according to the box instructions, ensuring it is al dente. It will finish cooking in the clam sauce. If you are using fresh pasta, be sure not to overcook it; it would be a shame to have gummy pasta!

Add the clams, white wine, basil, and parsley to the sauté pan. Season with a pinch of kosher salt. Cover the sauce with the lid until the clams begin to release their juices, about 4–6 minutes. You will hear them begin to pop open while they cook. Throw out any clams that don't open.

Once the pasta is al dente, reserve 1 cup of the starchy pasta water and pour it into the clam sauce.

Add the drained pasta to the sauté pan and continue to cook the pasta for another minute or two, stirring the pasta gently into the sauce.

Serve immediately into a large pasta bowl or straight into shallow individual bowls with an additional drizzle of olive oil, a few cracks of fresh black pepper, freshly grated parmesan, and another dash of red pepper flakes if you like.

SPINACH & DANDELION PIE WITH GOLDEN RAISINS & PINE NUTS

Serves 6–8

Extra-virgin olive oil

½ red onion, diced

1 medium leek, pale green and white
  end only, rinsed and minced

2–3 garlic cloves, minced

3 tablespoons dry white wine

2 bunches (about 8 oz) dandelion
  greens, roughly chopped with tough
  ends trimmed

8 oz (about 240 g) spinach,
  stems trimmed and roughly torn

1 handful flat-leaf parsley,
  roughly chopped

1 tablespoon fresh dill,
  roughly chopped

1 handful basil, roughly chopped

4–5 tablespoons fresh oregano,
  roughly chopped

⅓ cup (50 g) golden raisins, roughly
  chopped

¼ cup (15 g) pine nuts, minced

1 egg, lightly whisked

1 teaspoon kosher salt

½ teaspoon fresh cracked
  black pepper

8 oz (225g) fresh block feta in brine

½ cup (60 g) grated quality
  aged parmesan

Zest of one small lemon

1 tablespoon red pepper flakes

1 16-oz (454 g) package phyllo
  dough, room temperature

5 tablespoons poppy seeds

Bitter greens wrapped in a flaky phyllo crown with golden raisins and pine nuts make this a substantial vegetarian pie to serve for any summer feast. Vegetarians need not be forgotten at the weekend barbecue with this twist on the classic spanakopita. I'm not a vegetarian myself, but I've often found their options at most barbecues to be rather uninspired. The addition of white wine and fresh herbs make this classic a bit more interesting. This savory pie will please even the most reluctant of leafy green eaters.

Before beginning, make sure your dandelion greens and spinach are washed and patted dry, or else they will make the phyllo dough soggy. The easiest way to do this is to use a salad spinner or wrap them in paper towels and gently press them several times, like a little packet, and once more before combining them with the remaining ingredients.

In a large sauté pan, add 4–5 tablespoons of olive oil over medium-low heat and add the red onions and leeks. Sauté for about 8 minutes, stirring occasionally until soft and tender.

Add the garlic and the white wine to the pan. Continue to cook for another 3–5 minutes, stirring once or twice with a wooden spoon, and turn off the heat and set aside for now.

Preheat the oven to 350°F. Gather a 9" baking dish or springform pan. Drizzle a tablespoon of olive oil into the baking dish and coat it evenly along the sides and bottom.

In an extra-large bowl, combine the dandelion greens, spinach, parsley, dill, basil, oregano, golden raisins, and pine nuts. Try not to get too overwhelmed with the amount; it will be quite a lot to handle at first, but it will all cook down.

Add the sautéed red onions, leeks, and garlic to the greens bowl.

Whisk the egg and salt together with a few cracks of black pepper in a small bowl.

Thoroughly stir the egg to the greens mix.

Using your hands, break up the feta block into the bowl into small pieces and chunks. Continue to add the grated parmesan to the bowl.

Grate the lemon directly into the bowl, then add the red pepper flakes. Gently toss the mixture together until thoroughly combined; there will be many greens to handle so be sure to mix slowly to prevent spilling.

Gently roll out the phyllo dough so it lies flat on a clean work surface. You will only need 10–15 sheets, so you can wrap up the remainder in plastic wrap, set it in the fridge or freezer, and save it for another time.

Delicately take one sheet of phyllo dough and place it over the baking dish so that the two ends hang over about 2" over the rim. Phyllo is notoriously delicate and paper-thin, so handle it with care. It's okay if they break or tear; just nudge them back together and set back inside.

Drizzle a little olive oil over the layer and use your fingers or pastry brush to roughly coat the bottom and sides of the sheet.

Rotate the baking dish 180 degrees, take another sheet of the dough, and place it on the first layer, letting the two ends hang about 2" over the rim. It doesn't have to be exactly 180 degrees, but the idea is that you want the layer to cover the rim, so they are not stacked with an overhang only on two sides of the dish.

Continue these two steps with 10 more phyllo sheets. The baking dish rim should have a 2" overhang all around that eventually will be partially folded over.

Spoon the spinach and dandelion mixture into the baking dish, gently pressing it down into the center.

With your hands, take the ends hanging over the rim and bring them up to partially cover the sides of the spinach and dandelion mixture. Gently press the phyllo dough into a rough crust; it will not look neat, so no need to worry about that! It should look like a flaky, layered crown crust along the rim.

Add a tablespoon of water to a small dish, and using your pastry brush or finger, lightly brush or sprinkle the phyllo crust with water. Use more water if needed, just enough so that the poppy seeds will stick.

Sprinkle the poppy seeds evenly over the crust.

Bake the pie for 55–60 minutes until the crust is lightly golden and crisp.

Slice the pie into wedges in the baking dish or remove it from the springform pan and serve warm.

MAUI MAHI MAHI BURGER

Makes 6 burgers

6 4–5-oz sustainably caught mahi-
 mahi fillets with the skin removed
 (roughly one 1.5 lb fillet per person)

2 teaspoons ground cumin

2 teaspoons ground coriander

½ teaspoon garlic powder

Kosher salt

Extra-virgin olive oil

1 small pineapple, cored and cut
 into ¼" rounds

Tropics Slaw (recipe follows)

Winslow's Sweet Buns (recipe on
 page 121)

Cilantro & Poblano Aioli
 (recipe follows)

Toppings:

Butter lettuce

Heirloom tomato slices

Hot sauce

Avocado slices

Pickled red onions

One of the blessings of living on a pacific island is the abundance of fresh seafood. All around Hawaii, you'll find some version of a mahi-mahi burger, and for good reason too. It is a lighter and fresher option than a heavy beef burger. My version has a tropical slaw and a spicy aioli that gives a nice, creamy kick. If a tropical holiday isn't on the calendar this summer, bring it home with this taste of the islands. Sea bass, tuna, swordfish, or red snapper are delicious substitutions if fresh mahi-mahi is hard to come by at your local fishmonger. Sandwich the fish between Winslow's Sweet Buns, the following recipe.

Note: If you decide to serve both the slaw and aioli with the burgers, prep those first before you grill the fish and pineapple.

Preheat the grill to medium-high heat.

Place the fillets on a platter and generously drizzle each fillet with olive oil.

In a small bowl, combine the cumin, coriander, garlic powder, and a good pinch of salt and sprinkle it evenly over each fillet. Alternatively, you can simply sprinkle each spice directly onto each, followed by a healthy pinch of salt on both sides.

Place the cored pineapple rounds onto another plate and generously drizzle them with olive oil and a pinch of salt.

Once the grill is hot, place the fillets and pineapple rounds onto the grill and cover them. Grill the mahi-mahi for about 4–6 minutes on each side, flipping the fillets only once until they are flaky and opaque. Simultaneously grill the pineapple for 4–6 minutes on each side, flipping them once to maintain the striking grill marks. Keep an eye on these as they may take more or less time to get a nice char. Although, I've found that the fish and pineapple take roughly the same amount of time to grill.

Remove the fillets and pineapple from the grill and let them rest while you toast the soft buns. Brush a little olive oil on both bun halves and place them on the grill for 3–4 minutes until lightly toasted and golden. You can, of course, grill these at the same time as the fish and pineapple, depending on the size of your grill.

To assemble the burger, lay one fillet on the toasted bun and spoon a generous dollop of the aioli on top. Next, place one pineapple round per burger on top, followed by a spoonful of the tropic slaw, and continue to stack your favorite toppings, and then finish it off with second grilled bun half.

Cilantro & Poblano Aioli

¾ cup (about 170 g) extra-virgin olive oil–based mayonnaise

1 handful cilantro

2 tablespoons chopped poblano pepper (jalapeño works too if you like it spicier!)

1 garlic clove

Juice ½ lime

1 heaping tablespoon lime zest

1 teaspoon cumin

½ teaspoon kosher salt

¼ teaspoon cracked black pepper

Optional: A dash of hot sauce

In a food processor or blender, combine all the ingredients and blend until smooth, about 2–3 minutes. Taste and season with additional salt, hot sauce, or lime zest. When you are ready to assemble the burgers, serve the aioli into a small bowl with a spoon for your guests to help themselves. Refrigerate the aioli until serving, and any leftovers will keep for up to 5 days in the fridge.

WINSLOW'S SWEET BUNS

Makes 8–10 buns

1½ (350 ml) cups warm water

2¼ teaspoons (7 g) active dry yeast

½ cup (100 g) granulated white sugar

¼ cup (59 ml) vegetable oil

2 eggs + 1 egg yolk

5 cups (600 g) all-purpose flour

1 tablespoon kosher salt

Optional: Sesame seeds,
   Poppy seeds, Onion flakes

Homemade buns may seem like too much trouble to make, but they are truly incomparable to store-bought ones. Whenever we had a large family get-together for the 4th of July, fresh out of the oven would come the softest, pillowy golden buns you'd ever see. If you enjoy bread baking, give these a try. They hold up to a robustly stacked burger without getting soggy or flat. I like to slightly grill the cut face of each with a little olive oil before sandwiching them together. (These are aptly named for the nickname of my crumb thief.)

Combine the water, yeast, and sugar into a mixing bowl with a dough hook attached. Stir the mixture together until the yeast is dissolved. This dough is particularly sticky and soft, so I find it's best to use a mixer rather than kneading the dough by hand. Let the yeast mixture sit for 10 minutes until little bubbles form. If no activity is present, the yeast may be old or inactive. Repeat the process with new yeast.

Add the vegetable oil, 2 eggs, and 2 cups of flour and knead on medium speed for a minute or two until it's roughly combined. Scrape the sides of the bowl and continue to mix for another minute and then add in the salt.

Continue to add the remaining 3 cups of flour, one by one, slowly, on low speed, stopping several times to scrape down the sides of the bowl. It will be much softer than typical bread dough, so it needs added time to come together until it is a smooth and satiny ball of dough.

Once the dough starts to come away from the sides of the bowl and is springy to the touch, remove the hook (the dough may stick around the hook) and lightly oil another large bowl. Remove the dough and place it into the greased bowl, flipping it top-side up so both sides are lightly oiled, and cover it with plastic wrap.

Set the dough bowl to rise in a warm area in the house, not too hot but not drafty either, preferably on a sunny windowsill.

Allow the dough to rise for at least an hour until it's doubled in size.

Line a small baking sheet with parchment paper.

Once the dough is doubled in size and puffy, lightly dust a work surface with flour and scrape out the dough onto the table.

Divide it into roughly 8 or 10 (depending on how many you need) equal-sized balls with a bench scraper or simply eyeball it.

Shape each dough ball into a round bun, gently cupping the dough on the surface until it forms a plump bun. You can pinch the bottom together if need be, folding it into itself, and continue to shape it until it's a smooth ball. Lightly flatten them with a gentle pat of your hand.

Place each bun onto the baking sheet, leaving about 2" between each bun, and preheat the oven to 375°F. Let the buns rise in a warm place for at least 30 minutes until puffy, at least doubled in size, with a smooth surface. As they rise, they may touch each other, which is fine; just pull them apart when they come out of the oven.

Once the buns have roughly doubled in size, make a quick egg wash by whisking the yolk and a tablespoon of water together. Using a pastry brush, lightly brush the top of each bun evenly with the egg wash. If you want to add seeds or dried onion flakes, now is the time to sprinkle them over the egg wash on each bun.

Bake the buns for 20 minutes until golden and glossy.

Serve them warm or grilled lightly brushed with olive oil.

CARAMELIZED RED ONION & FENNEL TART

Serves 6–8

5 tablespoons unsalted butter,
  cut into chunks

3 medium red onions, cut into
  thin rounds

1 fennel bulb, thinly sliced with
  core removed

½ cup (118 ml) dry white wine

1½ teaspoons kosher salt

1 tablespoon fresh thyme leaves

1 cup (252 g) crème fraîche

¼ cup (20 g) goat cheese crumbles

1 tablespoon fresh chives, minced

¼ teaspoon ground mustard

1 sheet (245 g) quality, ready-made
  butter puff pastry, thawed

1 egg

1 teaspoon milk

1 tablespoon chopped walnuts

Any regular entertainer knows the magic and sheer ease of using quality pre-made puff pastry. Whip it out of the fridge or freezer, gather some cheese, onions, and herbs, and you're well on your way to a delicious meal. A delectable (and impressive-looking tart, I might add) tart appears out of seemly homely ingredients with the time-consuming folding and laminating left behind. Ho hum onions are usually bumping around in the dark in my pantry, and when caramelized with fennel and white wine, they are mouth-watering good. A rustic and simple vegetable tart like this one is another recipe you'll want to have in your recipe book for your outdoor table.

Preheat the oven to 425°F. Prepare a parchment-lined baking sheet.

In a large 10" sauté pan or Dutch oven over medium heat, add the butter chunks and swirl them around the pan until they begin to melt.

Add the red onion rounds and fennel to the pan. With a wooden spoon, gently stir the red onions and fennel, coating them with the melted butter. If you are having trouble managing it all, you can also work in two batches side by side.

Lower the heat slightly and let the red onions and fennel sweat, stirring only every few minutes to caramelize them, about 40 minutes total. They should be a nice golden brown and significantly wilted down. Be sure not to let them burn, and add a touch of water if needed.

Pour in the white wine, ½ teaspoon of kosher salt, and fresh thyme leaves to the mixture.

Cook for an additional 5 minutes on low, stir occasionally and then remove from heat. Set the mixture aside for now as you prepare the pastry.

On a lightly floured work surface, roll out the puff pastry sheet to roughly a 10" x 12" rectangle. You can, of course, roll it into a square—be sure it is ¼" thin. Place it on the baking sheet and let it firm up in the freezer for 15 minutes while you prepare the crème fraîche. This will ensure that it will be nice and flaky.

In a medium-sized bowl, combine the crème fraîche, goat cheese, fresh chives, ground mustard, and 1 teaspoon of kosher salt.

Once the puff pastry is chilled, remove it from the freezer and assemble the tart.

With a sharp knife, lightly score a 1" border around the outside to mark the crust. Prick the center a few times around with a fork.

For an extra golden crust, crack the egg with a tablespoon of milk in a small bowl and whisk together. Using a pastry brush or your finger, gently brush the border of the pastry with the egg wash.

Spread the crème fraîche filling evenly onto the center of the pastry, right up to the border.

Spoon the caramelized red onion s and fennel evenly over the filling.

Bake for 15–20 minutes until the bottom of the tart is golden brown.

Garnish with a few fresh thyme leaves and chopped walnuts.

This is best served warm straight from the oven while the pastry is crisp.

SICILIAN TUNA SPAGHETTI

Serves 4–6

1 1 lb (454 g) carton spaghetti or
    linguine

Extra-virgin olive oil

1 shallot, minced

1.5–2 lb (620 g) mixed cherry
    tomatoes (smaller halved and larger
    ones quartered)

2 garlic cloves, minced

1.5 oz (142 g) tin sustainably caught
    tuna in extra-virgin olive oil

1 cup (180 g) Kalamata or niçoise
    olives, pitted and roughly chopped

3 tablespoons caper berries

1 lemon

1 tablespoon lemon zest

1 bunch basil, roughly chopped

Kosher salt

Fresh cracked black pepper

Quality aged Pecorino Romano or
    parmesan, grated to serve

When I think of a dish that captures a Mediterranean summer holiday, this is it. Juicy ripe tomatoes, briny olives, oily tuna, and lots of lemon and olive oil are enticing nods to an idyllic holiday along the Sicilian coast. It reminds me of spending a summer traipsing around the cobbled streets along the Amalfi coast, drinking in the sun and sea. It's a quick pasta that comes together quickly with a few pantry staples and fresh ingredients. This is a favorite to serve for a summer dinner party with dry white wine and crusty bread.

Cook the pasta according to the carton's instructions, just shy of al dente in water as salty as the sea. The pasta will continue to cook in the sauce once tossed together.

In a large sauté pan, add a generous glug of olive oil and the shallots over medium-low heat. Once the pan warms, gently stir the shallots occasionally until soft and translucent, about 5–8 minutes.

Add tomatoes and cook for another 10 minutes until they are soft and slightly broken down. Gently press them with a wooden spoon to release their sweet juices. Season with a pinch of salt.

Add the garlic, cook on low for another 5 minutes, and then turn off the heat.

Once the pasta is cooked, reserve a cup of the starchy pasta water. Add the drained pasta with the reserved cup of water back to the pan with the tomato sauce.

Fork the drained tuna into the pasta, followed by the olives and capers. Squeeze in the juice of one lemon, add the lemon zest and a good handful of basil, reserving a small handful to sprinkle on the top.

Toss the pasta together in the sauté pan; it will take a few minutes to incorporate everything as it finishes cooking.

Taste and season with additional salt and a few cracks of fresh black pepper.

Once you transfer the pasta to your serving dish, sprinkle on the remaining torn basil and serve immediately.

GRILLED SAUSAGE SMORGASBORD

Serves 6

6 quality, sustainably raised
    bratwursts or Italian sausages

Toppings to follow

In our family, the entire summer season is speckled with cookouts, picnics, and backyard potlucks. It wouldn't be considered summer if the grill was not regularly fired up. You can't go wrong on the grill (besides burning it to a crisp), even if you don't consider yourself a regular home cook. These grilled sausages are easy, yet the variety of toppings make it an interesting alternative to the classic burger and hotdog. Set out these three spreads in separate bowls (alongside ketchup and mustard, of course) for your guests to help themselves to a relaxed backyard smorgasbord. If you can find quality brioche buns, all the better!

Preheat the grill to high heat or until coals are smoldering if using charcoal.

Grill the sausages until slightly charred and crisp, flipping once or twice. I like them a bit bubbly and charred. Regardless of your preference, the internal temperature should be at least 160°F.

Top the sausages with one of these delicious options and serve the sausages in a brioche bun or simply without.

Antipasti Relish

½ cup (roughly 75 g) Castelvetrano
    olives, pitted and finely minced

½ cup (roughly 75 g) Kalamata olives,
    pitted and finely minced

5 (55 g) marinated artichoke hearts,
    minced

4 pepperoncini, thinly sliced

2 slices fire-roasted red
    peppers, minced

Juice ½ lemon

1 small handful basil, minced

1 small handful flat-leaf
    parsley, minced

Pinch of kosher salt

Extra-virgin olive oil

Combine all the ingredients into a small bowl with a drizzle of olive oil until thoroughly mixed.

Roasted Grape Chutney

Extra-virgin olive oil

1 large shallot, minced

3 cups (585 g) ruby or concord grapes, cut in half

1 teaspoon red wine, such as a pinot noir or whatever you have opened

1 tablespoon quality aged balsamic vinegar

1 teaspoon fresh thyme leaves

½ teaspoon kosher salt

In a large sauté pan, add 2–3 tablespoons of olive oil and the shallots over medium heat. Cook the shallots, stirring once or twice for about 5–8 minutes until soft and translucent.

Add the grapes, a splash of red wine, balsamic vinegar, thyme leaves, and salt and cook for an additional 3–5 minutes over high heat. Reduce the heat down to a simmer, cover the pan and cook for another 35–45 minutes, stirring once or twice until the grapes break down and the mixture thickens. Remove the cover 5–10 minutes prior if there is additional liquid, and bring it up to medium heat for a few minutes until the chutney thickens.

This makes about 13 oz (370 g) and will last up to a week in the fridge if you don't use it all in one sitting.

Charred Purple Cabbage & Fennel Slaw

1 small purple cabbage, cored and cut into quarters (about 3 cups diced once grilled)

½ cup (65 g) fennel bulb, thinly sliced and diced

3 tablespoons extra-virgin olive oil–based mayonnaise

1 tablespoon extra-virgin olive oil

Juice ½ lemon

3 tablespoons flat-leaf parsley, minced

1 tablespoon fennel fronds, minced

½ teaspoon fresh oregano, minced

½ teaspoon kosher salt

Preheat the grill to high heat.

Brush each side of the cabbage quarters lightly with olive oil and place them flat side down onto the grill.

Grill each side of the cabbage quarters for 6–8 minutes until the outer face is nicely charred with grill marks. Remove the cabbage with tongs and let them slightly cool until you can handle them.

Finely slice and dice the cabbage into small ¼" pieces and combine it into a medium bowl with the fennel.

For the dressing, whisk mayonnaise, olive oil, lemon juice, parsley, fennel fronds, oregano, and salt in a small bowl until smooth and creamy.

Pour the dressing into the cabbage and fennel slaw and gently toss it together until evenly coated. Season with additional salt and black pepper to taste.

PROSCIUTTO-WRAPPED CHICKEN SKEWERS WITH FRESH PESTO

Serves 6

For the pesto:

1 large handful basil, washed
and dried

1 small handful arugula, washed
and dried

1 small handful oregano, washed
and dried

3 heaping tablespoons walnuts,
finely minced

2 garlic cloves, finely minced

1 heaping handful grated quality
aged parmesan

Extra-virgin olive oil

½ teaspoon kosher salt

Cracked black pepper to taste

For the chicken:

4–6 6-oz (roughly) boneless and skinless
chicken thighs (aim for 2 thighs per
person)

Extra-virgin olive oil

Kosher salt

3 tablespoons finely minced lemon rind

15 slices quality prosciutto di Parma

1 red onion, quartered and then cut
into chunks

2 handfuls cherry tomatoes

A rift on Jamie Oliver's summer classic, prosciutto-wrapped chicken skewers are a scrumptious alternative to old barbecue standbys. Basil is by far my favorite summer herb in the garden, and I love to make batches upon batches of variations of fresh pesto. You can easily swap in whatever additional herbs you have on hand—marjoram, parsley, mint, or even kale. Serve these crispy stuffed skewers alongside a platter of grilled garden vegetables for a laid-back midsummer feast.

Start by making the pesto by hand rather than using a food processor. It tastes much fresher, more vibrant. You can taste the subtleties in the flavors. Use a sharp chef's knife, which keeps the herbs from bruising and turning brown, and gather your herbs into a pile onto a large cutting board. Finely mince the herbs and add them to a small bowl.

Add walnuts, garlic, and parmesan to the herbs. Drizzle in a good glug of olive oil, about 5–6 tablespoons, until it becomes an even sauce. It shouldn't be swimming in oil but not too dry either.

Season with salt and black pepper to taste and set aside while preparing the chicken.

Preheat the grill to high heat, or if using charcoal, until the coals are smoldering.

Take each chicken thigh and place them on a clean surface and cover them with a layer of plastic wrap. Using a meat tenderizer or a can of beans, beat the chicken thighs down to tenderize and thin them out. They shouldn't be too thin or breaking apart but just enough so that they are about a third larger than before as it will be easier to roll up.

Cut each thigh into 2 to 3 equal strips. Place them on a plate with a good smattering of olive oil on both sides with a healthy pinch of salt to season them.

To assemble each stuffed chicken rollup, take one piece of flattened chicken and spoon a tablespoon of the pesto into the center with a pinch of the minced lemon rind. Roll the chicken lengthwise and wrap a piece or two of prosciutto around it. You may need to wrap them once or twice, depending on how stringy your prosciutto is.

Place the stuffed round onto a metal skewer and assemble the remaining rollups.

In addition to the chicken skewers, I like to include some tomatoes and onions or any summer veggies of your choice on additional skewers. Combine the tomatoes, onions, and veggies into a large bowl and drizzle them with olive oil and a good pinch of salt. Alternate adding the tomatoes and onions onto the skewers.

Place the skewers onto the hot grill. Grill the chicken skewers for about 6–7 minutes on each side, turning once. For extra certainty, use a thermometer to check the internal temperature of the chicken, which should register at least 165°F.

Grill the veggie skewers for about 8 minutes until lightly charred and crisp.

Serve the skewers immediately with additional pesto for dipping.

GRILLED FLATBREAD

Makes 6–8 individual flatbreads

For the dough:

2 ¼ (7 g) teaspoons active dry yeast

1 ¼ cup (295 ml) lukewarm water

3 cups (360 g) bread flour

½ teaspoon kosher salt

2 tablespoons extra-virgin olive oil

Topping Suggestions:

Cherry tomatoes

Arugula

Torn basil

Chopped olives

Prosciutto

Italian sausage

Zucchini blossoms

Artichoke hearts

Halved figs

Grilled peaches

Caramelized onions

Mozzarella

Quality aged pecorino Romano

Quality aged parmesan

Taleggio

Fontina

Burrata

Ricotta

Your choice of veggies[2]

The summer grill isn't just for your meats and veggies. Nearly one night a week in the summer growing up, we would slap pizza dough on the charcoal grill and load it up with whatever we had in the fridge or what was ripe in the garden. Once shaped, they cook up in mere minutes, leaving a nice crisp char. The beauty of this recipe is that it allows everyone to personalize their flatbread to their taste. The key is organizing the toppings beforehand and roughly knowing what combinations you're after. Invite friends over for an outdoor pizza party and allow them to contribute some of their favorite toppings—to each their own!

Dough

In a stand mixer with a dough hook or a large mixing bowl, combine the yeast and water. Stir the yeast until it is fully dissolved, and let it rest for 10 minutes. If the mixture shows no sign of activity or foamy bubbles, the yeast is no longer good. Repeat the process with fresh yeast.

At low speed, gradually add the flour cup by cup to the bowl. Mix until the flour is thoroughly combined, about 2 minutes.

Add the salt to the dough and mix it in for 1 minute at low speed. Let the dough rest for an additional 15 minutes.

Continue to knead the dough for 8–10 minutes on medium speed or with your hands on a floured work surface while gradually pouring in the olive oil until smooth and satiny.

Remove the dough from the bowl, place it in a lightly oiled bowl, and cover with plastic wrap or a tea towel. Allow the dough to rise in a warm spot in the house for about 1–2 hours, until it has doubled in size.

Once doubled in size, remove the dough from the bowl and place it on a lightly floured work surface.

Gather a parchment-lined baking sheet and decide the size and number of pizzas you would like to make. You can make either 6–8 individual flatbread or 2 larger rounds. Roughly cut out 6–8 balls of dough with a bench scraper.

Shape the dough on the parchment paper by patting it down on your hands with a drizzle of olive oil. It should be roughly ½"–1" thick. Flip the shaped flatbread over and brush the other side with olive oil.

» 2 *Any added veggies like zucchini, squash, potato, broccoli rabe, onions, and peppers should be pre-sautéed or grilled before adding as toppings.*

Continue to shape each flatbread and place them on the parchment paper on the baking sheet.

Let the shaped dough rest for at least 30 minutes while you prepare your toppings.

Gather all your toppings, sauces, and seasonings on a large tray (with spoons if needed) and place it right by your grill. It's easier to have everything prepared when you're at the grill, as they cook fast.

Once you are ready to grill, turn it on to medium-high heat.

Once the grill is at least up to 350°F or when the grills are nice and hot, using your hands, take a dough round and place it directly onto the grill. Be sure they are lightly brushed with oil. They may not be perfectly circular and look rustic, which is fine.

You must be quick about it; it's best to have all the flatbreads on the grill at the same time.

Let the flatbread grill for about 5 minutes on one side, but keep an eye on them, as the temperature may change. Close the grill to cook the pizzas for a minute or two. Brush the side facing up with more olive oil.

Peek underneath to check if they are a golden brown with a slight char.

Using a spatula or tongs, flip over the flatbreads all at once.

Immediately dress them with your selected toppings and seasonings like a normally baked pizza. Have fun with the toppings; there is no right or perfect combinations besides whatever you prefer!

Close the grill to melt any cheese for a minute or two.

Continue to grill for an additional 3–5 minutes. You may need to lower the grill if they are getting too crisp.

Remove the flatbreads from the grill onto a serving board and serve immediately. Add additional fresh herbs or seasonings if you like.

Here are two basic sauces to start as a foundation:

Basic Tomato Sauce

Extra-virgin olive oil
½ yellow onion, diced
2 garlic cloves, minced
1 28-oz (794 g) can diced tomatoes
1 tablespoon tomato paste
1 teaspoon dried oregano
1 tablespoon fresh chopped basil
½ teaspoon kosher salt
Cracked black pepper

In a large 10" sauté pan, add a glug of olive oil and onions over medium-low heat. Once the onions are translucent and soft, add in garlic, tomatoes, tomato paste, oregano, and basil. Bring the sauce down to a simmer and continue to cook for 8–10 minutes until it has slightly thickened, although the longer it simmers, the better. Season with salt and pepper to taste.

Arugula Basil Pesto

2 garlic cloves

½ cup (45 g) grated quality aged parmesan

½ cup (69 g) pine nuts or chopped walnuts

1 bunch fresh basil, about 1 cup

1 generous handful arugula

1 tablespoon lemon zest

1 cup (236 ml) extra-virgin olive oil

Pinch of kosher salt

Cracked black pepper to taste

In a food processor, add the garlic, grated parmesan, pine nuts, fresh basil, arugula, and lemon zest. Pulse several times until it resembles a rough paste. While pulsing, pour the olive oil in a steady stream until smooth. Stretch it or thin it with a tablespoon of water or additional olive oil. Season with salt and pepper to taste.

SUMMER GARDEN
ORECCHIETTE PASTA SALAD

Serves 6

1 lb (454 g) carton dry or fresh
    orecchiette pasta

⅓ cup (79 ml) pasta water

Extra-virgin olive oil

¼ red onion, diced

1 medium yellow squash, sliced into
    thin rounds (quarter the larger
    rounds), about 1½–2 cups (200 g)

1 medium zucchini, sliced into thin
    rounds (quarter the larger rounds),
    about 1½–2 cups (200 g)

1½ cups (about 265 g) halved
    cherry tomatoes

2 ears sweet corn, kernels removed

1 cup (100 g) fresh or frozen peas

Kosher salt

Juice of 1 lemon

1 bunch fresh basil, roughly chopped

Freshly cracked black pepper

Pecorino Romano shavings

With the overflowing piles of the garden's abundance, pasta is my go-to pantry staple to create a quick slapdash dish with everything but the hoe thrown in. I have never taken a liking to the mayo-based classic you'll find at nearly every 4th of July barbecue but prefer something fresher. Yellow squash, zucchini, and cherry tomatoes are some of the season's more abundant crops, making them ripe for the picking for an unassuming pasta salad with friends. This recipe is forgiving and intuitive, so feel free to improvise with what is fresh to you or ripe in your garden.

Boil the pasta to the package instructions in generously salted water, cooking to al dente, as it will finish cooking with the vegetables. Reserve ½ cup of the cooked pasta water.

In a large sauté pan, add 4 or 5 tablespoons of olive oil over medium-low heat.

Add the red onions, squash, zucchini, and cherry tomatoes to the pan. Stir occasionally and sauté until tender, about 10 minutes.

Add the corn and peas to the pan, combine everything, and cook for another 5 minutes on low heat.

Season with 1 teaspoon kosher salt and add the reserved pasta water.

Transfer the al dente pasta to the sauté pan with the vegetables, gently tossing everything together. Cook for another minute or so and taste the pasta.

Squeeze the juice of one lemon over pasta and add a generous handful of the chopped basil.

Gently toss everything together and season with an additional drizzle of olive oil, salt if necessary, and freshly cracked black pepper.

Serve immediately with Pecorino Romano shavings.

GRILLED STRIP STEAK WITH HAWAIIAN COFFEE RUB

Serves 4–6

4–6 ¼–½" thick (about 10–12 oz each) boneless New York strip steaks

½ cup (40 g) freshly ground unflavored coffee (I like a local Hawaiian one or choose your unflavored favorite)

2 tablespoons brown sugar

2 tablespoons kosher salt

1 tablespoon smoked paprika

1 tablespoon ground coriander

1 tablespoon cracked black pepper

¼ teaspoon garlic powder

¼ teaspoon ground mustard

Dash of cayenne pepper

Extra-virgin olive oil

For Salsa:

1 lb ripe pineapple, cored and cut into long spears

Extra-virgin olive oil

½ cup (about a handful) chopped cilantro

¼ red onion, diced

2 garlic cloves, minced

Dash of red pepper flakes

Juice of half a lime

Zest of half a lime

½ teaspoon kosher salt

Cracked black pepper to taste

Maui is home to the extra sweet Maui Gold pineapple, so naturally, I had to include a recipe inspired by our island's pride and joy. The traditional summer grilled steak gets a tropical refresher with a Hawaiian coffee rub and a juicy charred pineapple and lime salsa. I prefer to make my own rubs for grilling, and this one is a keeper for any backyard cookout. It presents beautifully and is a tasty dish for a fun and relaxed dinner party.

---

20 minutes before you fire up the grill, remove the steaks from the fridge and bring them up to room temperature.

Meanwhile, prepare the rub by combining the coffee, brown sugar, salt, smoked paprika, coriander, cracked black pepper, garlic powder, ground mustard, and cayenne pepper in a large mixing bowl.

Preheat the grill to high heat. Pat the steaks dry with a paper towel. Brush the steaks generously with olive oil.

Place one steak at a time in the coffee rub, spoon the rub over the steak, evenly coating both sides. Transfer them to a platter to take out to the grill.

Place the steaks onto the grill and cook until they are dark caramel brown, about 7–10 minutes on each side for medium-well, an internal temperature of 150°F (cook depending on your preference), 5–7 minutes on each side for medium-rare (130–140°F).

If you are also serving the pineapple salsa, place the pineapple wedges on the grill at the same time as the steak.

Remove the steaks from the grill and let them rest for a few minutes before thinly slicing them on a wood cutting board. Tent it with aluminum foil until you are ready to serve.

Grilled Pineapple & Lime Salsa

Place the pineapple spears into a large mixing bowl. Drizzle olive oil generously over them until they are evenly coated.

When grilling the steaks, place the pineapple spears on the grill and cook for 8–10 minutes until they have a nice toasty char with blackened grill marks. Turn them only once with tongs.

Remove them from the grill and let them cool completely.

Once cooled, dice them into ¼" chunks—the smaller, the better.

Place the diced pineapple into your serving bowl along with the cilantro, red onion, garlic, and red pepper.

Squeeze over the lime juice and add the zest. Add in a glug of olive oil and combine everything.

Season with salt and black pepper to taste. To serve, generously spoon over the salsa on the steak slices or place it separately in a bowl on the side and let your guests help themselves.

ROAST CHICKEN THIGHS WITH FIGS, OLIVES, & LEMON

Serves 6

For the marinade:

¾ cup (177 ml) extra-virgin olive oil

½ cup (118 ml) prosecco wine vinegar

1 cup (120 g) pitted Castelvetrano
   olives, roughly chopped

½ cup (75 g) pitted Kalamata olives,
   roughly chopped

2 garlic cloves, roughly chopped

½ cup (90 g) dried or fresh
   black mission figs

½ cup (90 g) dried or fresh
   California Calimyrna figs, halved

1 tablespoon caper berries

2 teaspoons kosher salt

3 bay leaves

1 teaspoon fresh oregano, minced

1 teaspoon fresh thyme leaves

¼ teaspoon ground black pepper

Dash of red pepper flakes

10–12 bone-in chicken thighs
   (skinless or with skin)

¼ cup (59 ml) dry white wine

3 lemons

Optional: 5–6 large Yukon gold
   potatoes, peeled and diced into
   large chunks
   3 tablespoons unsalted butter

This is one of those one-pan dishes that looks impressive, but you might as well have prepared it blindfolded—it's that easy. While most err on an Americana barbecue route for chicken for outdoor entertaining, I prefer a Mediterranean flavor. The dried figs soak up the succulent juices until they are plump and sweet. I adore olives in just about everything and paired with the wine, capers, lemon, and herbs they add a distinctive salty flavor to the moist chicken thighs. I've also included diced potatoes as an optional addition. They are always the perfect pairing for a good roast chicken, albeit a light summery choice. Choose a crisp, dry white wine and olive focaccia to round off the table.

Add the chicken thighs to a large gallon Ziploc bag. Continue to add all the marinade ingredients into the bag.

Gently shake and turn the bag to ensure that every piece of chicken is thoroughly coated with the marinade. Let the chicken marinate in the fridge overnight or for at least 6 hours. Once you are ready to roast, preheat the oven to 425°F and gather a large roasting tray or large cast-iron skillet.

Transfer the chicken thighs and all the marinade into the roasting tray or skillet, arranging the thighs skin side up in a single layer. Nestle the figs and olives around the thighs and pour in the wine. Slice the lemons into wedges, squeeze one or two around the dish, and tuck in the remaining.

If you are including the potatoes, tuck them in around the chicken thighs and lightly coat them with the marinade or an additional drizzle of olive oil and a sprinkle of kosher salt. Roast the chicken thighs for 35–40 minutes, basting the chicken with the juice every 15 minutes, and turn the potatoes.

Once the chicken is cooked through and the potatoes are slightly crisp and tender, transfer the chicken thighs and potatoes to a serving platter. Use a slotted spoon to transfer the olives, figs, and capers on top of the chicken thighs, leaving the remaining juices.

For an additional sauce, add the pan juices to a sauté pan or simply use the same cast-iron skillet over medium heat, scraping any brown bits up from the bottom of the pan. Continue to cook the juices until they reduce by half, and then add the butter, whisking the sauce constantly until the butter is melted. Taste and season with salt and pepper. Serve the sauce on the side to spoon it over the chicken. You also can simply bring the whole tray or skillet to the table and serve it with tasty focaccia or ciabatta on the side.

BUTTERNUT SQUASH & APPLE LASAGNA WITH BÉCHAMEL SAUCE

Serves 6–8

6 strips (170 g) organic, free-range applewood smoked uncured bacon, diced

2 large yellow onions, diced

1 eating apple (Cortland or honey crisp), peeled and diced

1 tablespoon fresh sage, minced

1 small butternut squash, diced into ½" pieces (about 2 cups)

2 cups (473 ml) whole milk

6 tablespoons unsalted butter

3 tablespoons all-purpose flour

2 cups (roughly 470 g) extra sharp cheddar cheese

1½ teaspoons kosher salt

1½ teaspoons freshly cracked black pepper

2 cups (500 g) whole milk ricotta cheese

1 egg

1 teaspoon ground nutmeg

1 teaspoon red pepper flakes

1 cup (89 g) grated quality aged parmesan

12 lasagna oven-ready sheets or dry noodle sheets

1 8-oz bag (227 g) baby spinach

1 tablespoon chopped walnuts

When summer is coming to an end and the air starts to feel crisp, I find myself starting to crave warmer and heartier dishes. The turn of seasons from the gloriously sunny summer days to the brisk and colorful autumn also marks the harvest season. Lasagna is one of my favorite comfort foods and with autumnal flavors like apple, butternut squash, caramelized onions, and smoked bacon in a creamy béchamel sauce, it satisfies that craving for something hearty and nourishing. Gather the blankets and call over some hungry friends for a cozy fall evening by the firepit.

Preheat the oven to 375°F and gather a 9" x 13" lasagna or casserole dish.

Add the pieces of bacon and onion to a large Dutch oven over medium-low heat and stir frequently until the bacon fat begins to render and the onions become soft and translucent, about 5 minutes. Once the bacon is slightly crisp, lower the heat and continue to cook, stirring occasionally, until the onions caramelize and are light brown. Season with a pinch of salt.

Stir in the diced apple and sage into the bacon and onion mix, cooking the apples until they are tender but not mushy, about 5 minutes. Turn off the heat and set aside to prepare the squash and béchamel sauce.

Add the butternut squash to a small pot with enough water to cover and cook until an inserted knife goes through without resistance. Once tender, drain and run the butternut squash under cold water for a minute or so and set aside. To make the béchamel sauce, warm the milk in a small saucepot, bring it to a low simmer, and then turn off the heat.

In another sauté pan, melt the butter over low heat and gradually add the flour, continually whisking until it becomes a roux or wet paste. While whisking, pour in the warmed milk and continue to whisk over low heat until the milk is thoroughly combined and any lumps are removed.

Add 1½ cups of the cheddar cheese to the roux and gently melt the cheese until thoroughly incorporated into a creamy sauce. Season with ½ teaspoon of kosher salt and ½ teaspoon of black pepper. Taste and season with additional salt if necessary and set the sauce aside over a simmer to prepare the filling.

For the filling, combine the ricotta in a large mixing bowl with the egg, nutmeg, red pepper flakes, parmesan, and the remaining cheddar cheese. Season with ½ teaspoon of salt and a few cracks of black pepper.

If using dry lasagna noodles, cook them according to the box instructions until al dente. The oven-ready lasagna sheets do not need to be cooked beforehand. To assemble the lasagna, spread a few tablespoons of the béchamel sauce to the bottom of the casserole dish.

Layer 3 sheets of the lasagna noodles side by side on top of the sauce. Spread two tablespoons of the bacon and onion mixture evenly over the noodles. Spoon a tablespoon or two of the béchamel sauce over the bacon and onions. Sprinkle over two tablespoons of the cooked butternut squash over the bacon and onions. Take a small handful of the spinach and scatter it over the butternut squash. Follow by spreading two tablespoons of the ricotta mix over the spinach. Top with another layer of lasagna noodles and repeat the process until you have 4 equal layers.

Once the lasagna is fully assembled, spread the remaining béchamel sauce evenly over the top of the noodles. Sprinkle with chopped walnuts, additional grated cheddar or parmesan, and cracked black pepper.

If using the oven-ready noodle sheets, bake for 60 minutes until the top is golden and bubbling. If using cooked lasagna sheets, bake for 40–45 minutes until golden and bubbling. If the top is browning too quickly, cover with aluminum foil in the last 15 minutes of baking. Let the lasagna cool for 15 minutes before serving with a crusty baguette or ciabatta.

SWEET DELIGHTS

I've always been a fresh fruit and cream kind of girl instead of a cloyingly sweet confection. During the warmer months, I gravitate toward light and fruity desserts. Sometimes even a few wedges of cheese and fresh fruit slices are lovely to serve after a summery dinner party. I love to bake, but I wouldn't say I have a sweet tooth; usually a chunk of extra dark chocolate with raspberries after dinner hits the mark for me. Although, it is hard to say no to a homemade sweet! Many of these recipes were inspired by my garden. Growing up on our Vermont farm, we were blessed with bushels and bushels of berries, particularly blueberries that popped into our mouths by the handful, eating to our hearts' content. Ripe fruit is an equally sweet rival to the richest of cakes! Crisps, cobblers, and fruit pies are some of our family's favorites for the summer months. The recipes you'll find in this section celebrate the seasonal sweet delights, such as the Berries in Lemony Syrup with Buttermilk Biscuits on page 185, or the Strawberry and Peach Crisp on page 167 alongside a tempting and oh-so-fudgy skillet brownie for the chocolate lovers, of course. Lest we forget chocolate! The Pistachio and Cherry Affogato on page 169 comes together with a snap of a finger and feels so whimsical as if you're sitting alongside Alice at the Mad Hatter's table. Serving a little something sweet isn't necessary, but these no-fuss recipes certainly will make it more pleasurable. The summer season is blissfully sweet on its own, but who doesn't like to indulge with friends in the sunshine?

WHIPPED MASCARPONE WITH STRAWBERRIES & AMARETTO

Serves 4

½ cup (113 g) mascarpone
2 tablespoons granulated white sugar
½ cup (118 ml) heavy whipping cream
1 teaspoon pure vanilla extract
Kosher salt
Juice of half a lemon
¼ cup (53 g) golden brown sugar
1 cup (166 g) strawberries, quartered
1 tablespoon unsalted pistachios,
    roughly chopped
Amaretto (I prefer Disaronno)

With just a few key ingredients, this delightful dessert can be whipped up at a moment's notice for a balmy summer evening. Berries and cream are a quintessential summer pairing. It reminds me of wildflower fields, lazy days in the sunshine, and green meadows. A splash of amaretto enhances the sweetness of the strawberries in a tempting way.

In a large mixing bowl or a stand mixer with a whisk attachment, combine the mascarpone, white sugar, heavy cream, vanilla extract, and a pinch of kosher salt.

Whisk the mascarpone mixture for about 3 minutes on medium speed until it forms soft, yet firm peaks. Place the bowl in the fridge until you are ready to assemble.

Add the quartered strawberries into a large mixing bowl with the golden-brown sugar and a pinch of salt. Using a wooden spoon, coat the strawberries evenly with the sugar.

Squeeze half a lemon over the strawberries, stirring until thoroughly combined.

Gather four mason jars or teacups to serve. Place roughly 2 tablespoons of the chilled mascarpone cream into each jar. Add a spoonful of the strawberries to each glass on top of the cream and then top it off with another spoonful of the mascarpone cream.

Pour a tablespoon of amaretto (you can use as little or more as you like) over the mascarpone cream into each jar.

Add a pinch of chopped pistachios over the mascarpone cream to finish.

GRAPEFRUIT &
ROSEMARY CHEESECAKE

Serves 6–8

For the crust:

1 8-oz package (220 g) shortbread biscuits

1 cup (125 g) whole pecans

¼ teaspoon rosemary, minced

¼ teaspoon kosher salt

7 tablespoons unsalted butter, melted

For the filling:

4 8-oz (904 g) packages whole-fat cream cheese, softened to room temperature

1 cup (240 g) whole-fat sour cream, room temperature

1½ cups (297 g) granulated white sugar

1 heaping teaspoon pink grapefruit zest

¼ teaspoon kosher salt

4 eggs, room temperature

2 egg yolks

1 tablespoon pure vanilla extract

1 tablespoon pink grapefruit juice

¼ cup (59 ml) heavy whipping cream

For the topping:

1 cup (236 ml) heavy whipping cream, cold

¼ cup (50 g) granulated white sugar

1 tablespoon pure vanilla extract or vanilla bean paste

1 pink grapefruit, sliced into half-moons

Rosemary sprigs to garnish

This cheesecake is a light and luscious dessert for a sublime summer evening. The hint of rosemary is an unexpected yet delicious pairing with the sharp grapefruit. Apart from the gorgeous coral color adorning the creamy top, the fresh grapefruit curd cuts the sweetness with a vibrant zing spooned over this summery cake.

Preheat the oven to 350°F. Line the bottom of a 9" springform pan with parchment paper and lightly grease the sides of the pan.

To make the crust, add the shortbread biscuits and pecans to a food processor and blitz for 2–3 minutes until it resembles fine crumbs.

Transfer the biscuit crumbs to a small bowl and add the rosemary, salt, and melted butter. Combine the mixture with a spoon until the crumbs are evenly coated with butter.

Spread the biscuit mixture into the base of the pan, pressing it firmly down into every corner to create an even layered crust about ¼"–½" thick. I prefer not to press it onto the sides of the pan as it's likely to be uneven.

Set the pan into the fridge to chill while preparing the filling.

In a stand mixer with a paddle attachment, add the cream cheese and sour cream into the bowl. Whip on medium-low speed until creamy and smooth.

Continue to add the sugar and mix on high until fully incorporated, scraping down the sides of the bowl.

Add the grapefruit zest and salt and mix on medium speed until thoroughly incorporated and smooth. Be sure to scrape down the sides of the bowl.

Add the vanilla, grapefruit juice, and one egg at a time, followed by the yolks and heavy cream, mixing at low speed after each addition and scraping down the sides of the bowl. Be careful not to mix at high speed because it will create a denser cake, so once the eggs and heavy cream are added, I prefer to continue to slowly whisk the mixture together by hand until smooth and evenly incorporated. This ensures that the texture is light and airy.

Pour the batter into the pan on top of the crust, smoothing the top with a rubber spatula.

Gather a roasting pan, fill it with 2" of boiling water, and gently place the cake pan into the water. Alternatively, if it's easier, you can set the cheesecake pan in the roasting pan and then pour in the boiling water afterward.

Bake the cheesecake for 1 hour 15 minutes until the top is set except for a soft center. It should have a slight jiggle in the center when you gently shake the pan. If it browns too quickly, simply cover it with aluminum foil.

To prevent cracking, once the cheesecake is finished, turn off the oven and prop the oven door open with a wooden spoon and let it cool completely inside. A dramatic temperature change creates cracks on the surface, so a little patience goes a long way! Once the cake has cooled, gently remove it from the pan and place it on your serving plate. I find it's easier to do once it's completely cooled, so allow it to chill for at least 4 hours in the fridge before serving.

Meanwhile, prepare the topping by adding the chilled heavy cream into the large mixing bowl of a stand mixer with a whisk attachment or a bowl if using a hand mixer.

Whisk the heavy cream together on high until it thickens, then add the sugar and scraped vanilla beans. Continue to whisk the cream together until it forms billowy but firm peaks. Set the bowl straight into the fridge until the cake is completely chilled.

Once the cheesecake is chilled, gently spread dollops of whipped cream on top. Fan out the grapefruit slices in a rose-like fashion or whatever looks pretty to you with a few sprigs of rosemary tucked in the side.

Serve chilled with additional cream, a spot of grapefruit curd (recipe follows), sauvignon blanc, or dry champagne.

Fresh Grapefruit Curd

1 cup (236 ml) ruby red grapefruit juice (either freshly squeezed or store-bought)
2 tablespoons grapefruit zest
½ cup (100 g) granulated white sugar
3 egg yolks
6 tablespoons unsalted butter, cut into chunks
½ teaspoon kosher salt

In a medium saucepan over low-medium heat, add the grapefruit juice, zest, sugar, and egg yolks.

Continually whisk until the curd begins to look smooth and even. If the curd isn't thickening, turn up the heat slightly and continue to whisk.

Once it reaches a smooth and thicker consistency, lower the heat and add the butter. Using a rubber spatula, gently stir the butter into the curd until completely melted. Season with salt. Taste and add additional sugar if necessary. It tends to be tarter if using freshly squeezed juice.

The curd will thicken as it cools; it should be spreadable like a jam. Once it is completely cooled, drizzle it on each cut slice. I like to store the extra curd in an old jam or mason jar in the fridge where it will last about a week.

OH LÀ LÀ TIRAMISU

Serves 6

8 oz (227 g) mascarpone

1 heaping tablespoon orange zest

1 cup (236 ml) heavy whipping cream, chilled

1 teaspoon pure vanilla extract

½ cup (100 g) granulated white sugar

1 cup (236 ml) rosé (for a nonalcoholic version, use orange juice)

Optional: 1 tablespoon elderflower cordial or Cointreau

1 7-oz package 24 Savoiardi biscuits (ladyfingers)

3 tablespoons unsweetened cocoa powder

1 lb (454 g) strawberries, hulled and thinly sliced

4–5 tablespoons strawberry jam

1 oz (30 g) piece dark chocolate, grated

Think of this as the fruity counterpart to the classic tiramisu. A blush rosé is the darling wine of the summer months, and paired with luscious cream, scarlet strawberries, and sweet ladyfingers, it is simply perfection. It's a fanciful and cheery dessert that Marie Antoinette would no doubt serve for one of her frivolous summer parties right alongside the champagne. Pop open the bubbly!

In a stand mixer with a whisk attachment, add the mascarpone, orange zest, and ¼ cup of sugar into the bowl. Whisk on high for a few minutes until velvety and soft. Scrape the mascarpone into another small bowl and set aside.

Wipe out the same mixing bowl and pour in the heavy cream. Whisk on high for a minute or two, and when slightly thickened, add the vanilla and remaining sugar and continue to whisk for 2–3 minutes until it forms billowy but firm peaks.

Scrape the mascarpone with a rubber spatula gently into the whipped cream, folding it in until spreadable and smooth. Set the bowl inside into the fridge while preparing the biscuits.

Gather a glass 8" x 8" baking dish, or a 9" round cake tin works perfectly fine too.

Pour in the rosé and any added liqueur into a shallow bowl.

The assembly of the tiramisu should happen quickly, so have the cream, cocoa powder, strawberries, jam, and dark chocolate ready.

Sift over a tablespoon or two of the cocoa powder on the base of the dish.

Take one ladyfinger and dip it into the wine for a mere second, flipping it with your finger or a fork to coat both sides. Pull it out as fast as you can as the biscuits can get soggy and too boozy otherwise!

Place the biscuit into the dish and continue the process until the first base layer is complete, with the biscuits arranged side by side.

For the filling, spoon half of the mascarpone cream over the biscuits, spreading it evenly over the base layer.

Add a few dollops of strawberry jam over the mascarpone cream, spreading evenly.

Place roughly half of the strawberry slices side by side over the jam, covering the entire base and tucking in any little bits or ends. (If using orange juice, dust over an additional layer of cocoa powder here.) The remaining slices will be added to the top layer.

Continue to dip the remaining biscuits and place them side by side on top of the strawberry layer to finish.

Follow the same steps of layering the mascarpone cream, jam, and strawberries. Let the tiramisu set in the fridge for at least 4 hours or overnight to allow all the flavors and textures to meld together. (If in a time pinch, stick it in the freezer for 30 minutes to help it set.)

When you're ready to serve, add a few generous dollops of additional whipped cream on top with a couple of whole strawberries and a smattering of freshly grated orange zest and shavings of dark chocolate. Serve chilled with a nice floral glass of rosé, of course!

FARM STAND STRAWBERRY & PEACH CRISP

Serves 6

For the filling:

4 ripe medium-sized peaches

1 lb (500 g) strawberries, hulled and
  quartered

1 cup (207 g) packed light golden-
  brown sugar

½ tablespoon all-purpose flour

Juice of one lemon

¼ teaspoon kosher salt

For the crumb:

2½ cups (240 g) old fashioned
  rolled oats

8 tablespoons unsalted butter, softened

¼ cup (40 g) all-purpose flour

¼ cup (59 ml) wildflower honey or ¼
  cup (55 g) light golden-brown sugar

½ teaspoon kosher salt

¼ teaspoon ground cinnamon

¼ teaspoon ground ginger

A fresh fruit crisp with apples, berries, or stone fruit is a homely yet scrumptious dessert for an outdoor gathering. Warm strawberries and peaches topped with a crisp, spiced crumble remind me of summers on the farm; it was our go-to dessert all season long. We would eat the entire dish in just one sitting with grass-stained feet and sticky fingers. It's a humble dessert, but by using the season's best fruit, it is as fit for royalty as it is for a few country bumpkins.

Preheat the oven 350°F. Gather a 9" x 9" baking dish.

To peel the peaches, bring a large stockpot with water up to a boil. Score the bottom of the peaches with an *X* and fill a large bowl with ice water.

Place the peaches in the boiling water for only 30 seconds, and then with a slotted spoon, immediately place them into the bowl of ice water in the sink under cold running water.

Using a small knife or your fingers, peel back the skin of the peaches, starting by the *X*. They should come off easily.

Cut the peaches in half and remove the pit. Slice the peaches into half-moons and then into small cubes. They should be roughly the same size as a quartered strawberry.

In your baking dish, thoroughly combine the peaches, strawberries, sugar, flour, lemon juice, and salt until evenly coated. Let the filling sit for 15 minutes while preparing the crumb topping.

In a separate bowl, combine the oats, butter, flour, honey or sugar, salt, cinnamon, and ginger.

Using your fingers (which I find is the easiest way), work the butter into the oat mixture until it forms small rough clumps and is evenly distributed throughout.

Spoon the crumb mixture evenly over the fruit filling.

Bake the crisp for 40–45 minutes until the crisp is lightly golden and fruit juices bubble around the edges.

Let the crisp cool for 10 minutes, and then serve with fresh vanilla bean or pistachio ice cream (essential!).

PISTACHIO & CHERRY AFFOGATO

Serves as many as desired.

Pistachio gelato

Cherry ice cream
(preferably with chunks of fruit)

Salted caramel (recipe follows)

Cacao nibs

Cherries

Roasted and unsalted pistachios,
    roughly chopped

Shortbread or biscotti to serve

Espresso

Salted Caramel:
Makes 1 13-oz (370 g) jar

1 cup (200 g) granulated white sugar

6 tablespoons salted butter, cut into
    chunks

½ cup (118 ml) heavy whipping cream

1 teaspoon kosher salt

This is another "trick up the sleeve" Italian recipe for dinner parties. Gather some lovely little teacups or mugs, a bit of gelato, your favorite toppings, and pour-over hot espresso or coffee. It's a great last-minute dessert idea for a lively evening and looks elegant with a little crispy biscuit tucked in on the side. Pistachio and cherry are two of my favorite flavors that always are a knockout topped with salted caramel and cacao nibs.

This recipe is more about assembly rather than exact quantities. It is up to your liking and preferences, making it easier and fun.

Gather as many bowls as you need to serve. I like to use teacups as they are sweet and add a decorative, elegant flourish to an otherwise simple dessert.

Prepare the espresso as you would normally for as many guests as you have.

Add two or three scoops of the pistachio gelato or cherry ice cream into each teacup.

For the pistachio version, I love it topped with salted caramel and chopped pistachios. If you prefer a cherry option, try it with cacao nibs and whole cherries on top. The possibilities are endless!

Once the espresso is ready, bring the teacups with ice cream to the table and pour a splash of espresso in each. I like to give my guests the choice to add as much as they like or none at all. You know there is always one in the party that likes a good espresso after dinner and another that won't be able to sleep a wink! (I'm in the won't-sleep-a-wink camp!)

Serve immediately with shortbread or a biscotti on the side.

Salted Caramel

In a clean heavy-duty saucepan over medium heat, add the sugar and consistently stir with a rubber spatula until it begins to melt and thicken. Try not to let the mixture splatter on the side of the pan. It will eventually melt down to a golden-brown color. Keep an eye on it if it burns or heats too quickly. The key is to keep gently stirring until fully melted.

Once the sugar has completely melted down, add in the butter chunks and continuously stir as the sugar will naturally bubble and boil when you add the butter. If the butter begins to separate from the sugar, immediately remove it from the heat and whisk until combined. The sugar may clump and crystallize at this stage, so keep that in mind; remove it from the heat and keep stirring vigorously.

When the butter is completely melted, let the mixture cook for a minute without stirring.

Slowly pour the heavy cream while simultaneously whisking. It may splatter due to the temperature difference between the cold cream and hot caramel. Gently stir the heavy cream into the caramel until thoroughly combined.

Remove the caramel from the heat and stir in the salt. Let the caramel slightly cool, as it will thicken. You can reheat it on the stove over low heat if you like before pouring it over the pistachio affogato or any dessert. It will keep in the fridge in an airtight jar for up to two weeks if you don't use it all in one evening.

KULA BLACKBERRY TART

Serves 6

For the pastry:

¼ cup (28 g) roasted unsalted
   pistachios

1½ cups (180 g) all-purpose flour

¼ cup (28 g) powdered sugar

Pinch of salt

8 tablespoons unsalted butter, softened
   and cut into chunks

1 egg yolk (save the whites)

¼ cup (59 ml) ice water, plus a few
   tablespoons more if needed

For the filling:

1¼ cups (120 g) almond flour

¼ cup (30 g) all-purpose flour

8 tablespoons unsalted butter, softened

¼ cup (50 g) granulated white sugar

¼ teaspoon kosher salt

1 egg

Reserved egg white

1 tablespoon pure almond extract

1 teaspoon grated lemon zest

4–5 tablespoons blackberry jam

1 handful ripe blackberries

¼ cup (17 g) slivered almonds

Powdered sugar for dusting

Fresh berries are one of summer's finest delights. Berry picking is one of my favorite seasonal activities, plucking handfuls into my basket as I work down the rows while Winslow nibbles on the lower hanging berries. When the wild blackberries are in season, I love to make this twist on the classic Bakewell tart. Blackberries are one of the season's juiciest berries with a deep violet color. It's an elegant yet easy dessert for a dinner party at the peak of summer. Don't forget a scoop of ice cream on top!

To make the pastry, add the pistachios to a food processor and blitz for 2–3 minutes until finely ground.

In a large mixing bowl, combine the ground pistachios, flour, powdered sugar, and salt.

Add the butter pieces into the dry mixture and cut in the butter with a pastry cutter or your hands until it resembles coarse, pea-size crumbs.

Continue to add the yolk and ice water into the dough and roughly stir it together with a rubber spatula. It will look like a wet shaggy mess with dry bits at this point.

Now pour the rough dough onto a lightly floured work surface and cup it with your hands into a smooth, cohesive ball. You may need one or two more tablespoons of ice water to bring the dough together. Be careful not to knead or overwork it; just form the dough until it comes together with the dry bits incorporated to form an even dough.

Place the dough ball right back into the mixing bowl and set it in the freezer for at least 30 minutes. The dough will be easier to handle and roll out once it's chilled.

Preheat the oven to 375°F and gather a circular 9" nonstick fluted tart tin.

Meanwhile, begin to prepare the filling by combining, in another mixing bowl, the almond flour, all-purpose flour, butter, sugar, and salt.

Whisk together the egg and reserved egg white until light and foamy. Continue to add the almond extract and lemon zest into the eggs.

Gently pour the egg mixture into the dry ingredients, incorporating everything into a smooth and creamy paste. Set the mix aside in the fridge while rolling out the dough.

Remove the chilled dough from the freezer onto a lightly floured work surface.

Roll out the dough to roughly ¼"-thick circles roughly 12"–13" in diameter. With each roll, flip the circle over and lightly dust the surface and the dough with flour, as it does get sticky. For a better measurement, place the tin on top of the rolled dough to understand how much more or less you need to roll.

Gently place the rolled dough into the tin. There may be an inch or two of overhang along the edge. Before you cut away anything, be sure to press the dough well into every crevasse and corner. I like to run my fingers along the tart rim, gently pressing the dough into the fluted sides.

Gently fold any overhang over the rim of the tin. For a quick way to trim off any excess dough, roll the rolling pin over the rim of the tin. It will cleanly cut away the extra dough for a nice finish.

With any extra dough, patch up any thinner areas and roll out a small ball of dough to continue to press the base of the dough into the fluted sides. Prick the base with a fork several times around.

To par-bake the dough, once you've rolled it into the tin, line it with parchment paper, leaving a generous overhang.

Fill the lined tin with old, dried beans or pie weights, ensuring that every corner is filled.

Bake the tart case for 15 minutes, then remove it from the oven. Gently remove the beans or pie weights and parchment paper.

Spread a few tablespoons of the blackberry jam evenly over the base of the tart case.

Take out the filling from the fridge and spoon it over the jam evenly with a rubber spatula.

Sprinkle the blackberries over the filling, gently nestling them on top.

Continue to sprinkle the slivered almonds evenly over the tart.

Bake for 35–40 minutes until the crust is a light golden brown and when a knife inserted in the center of the filling comes out clean.

Let the tart cool 10 minutes before removing it from the tin.

Once it has completely cooled, lightly dust the top with powdered sugar.

Serve with fresh blackberries, ice cream, or whipped almond cream!

LEMON CAKE WITH FRESH LEMON CURD & BLUEBERRIES

Serves 6–8

3 cups (360 g) all-purpose flour

2½ teaspoons baking powder

½ teaspoon baking soda

½ teaspoon kosher salt

1½ cups (330 g) granulated white sugar

16 tablespoons unsalted butter, softened

4 eggs, room temperature

1 tablespoon pure vanilla extract

Juice of 2 lemons

1 tablespoon lemon zest

1 cup (240 ml) buttermilk, room temperature

Heaping handful of blueberries

Fresh mint to garnish

Picking a basket full of cheery lemons in my garden is a painting of summer. Lemons are refreshing, light, and sharp, making them an excellent flavor choice for warm weather. This citrusy cake is perfect for a birthday or other celebratory occasion. If you are in a pinch, you can use store-bought lemon curd, although nothing quite compares to a homemade one. Topped with fresh blueberries and cream, it looks like sunshine on a cloudless blue summer's day.

Preheat the oven to 350°F. Grease two 9" springform bottom cake tins.

Sift flour, baking powder, baking soda, and salt in a large bowl.

Using either a stand mixer with a paddle attachment or handheld electric one, cream together the sugar and butter for 2–3 minutes until smooth (it still will be a little grainy).

Add the eggs, one at a time, at a low speed, beating well after each addition. The mixture should be light and airy.

Continue to add in the vanilla, lemon juice, and lemon zest.

At low speed, gradually add in the previously sifted dry ingredients. Scrape down the sides of the bowl to ensure it is properly combined.

Slowly pour in the buttermilk while mixing at low speed until it reaches a smooth batter.

Pour in the batter, evenly divided between each tin.

Bake for 30–35 minutes until golden brown or when an inserted knife comes out clean. Let the cakes sit for 10 minutes in the tin before removing them onto a cooling rack.

Prepare the whipped cream and lemon curd while the cakes cool completely.

When assembling the cake, use a sharp serrated knife to level off the two domes so they are flat and even. This will make them easier to stack when you begin to layer them.

Decide if you would like a two-layer or four-layer cake. I opt for two as it's easier to construct.

Continue to cut the two cake rounds in half if you want a four-layer cake. To cut the cake evenly, I like to use four toothpicks inserted into the middle of the sides of each round as a guide. Gently cut the cakes in half with the knife, guiding it with the toothpicks around the edges and finally through the center.

Gather your cake platter or stand and place one cake round in the center.

Spoon a generous layer of curd on top of the first sponge, not too thick but 3 or 4 tablespoons worth. For a two-layer cake, continue to add dollops of whipped cream spread over the curd.

Gently place the second sponge on top of the curd and cream.

Spoon a generous amount of whipped cream on top of the cake.

Scatter a heaping handful or two of fresh blueberries and mint to garnish. Any edible flowers, such as chamomile, would be lovely to add too! I like to make it look lush and inviting with lots of berries spilling over.

Tip: On a warm day, once you assemble the cake, immediately stick it into the fridge until you are ready to decorate. Also inserting a small wooden dowel or wooden skewers through the layers will help to stabilize the cake if it's wobbly. You can have a bowl of whipped cream on the side as well.

Fresh Lemon Curd

Juice of one large lemon
2 tablespoons lemon zest
½ cup (100 g) granulated white sugar
3 egg yolks
6 tablespoons unsalted butter, cut into chunks
½ teaspoon kosher salt

In a medium saucepan over low-medium heat, add the lemon juice, zest, sugar, and yolks.

Continually whisk until the curd begins to look smooth and even. If the curd isn't thickening, turn up the heat slightly and continue to whisk.

Once it reaches a smooth and thicker consistency, lower the heat, and add in the butter. Using a rubber spatula, gently stir the butter into the curd until it is completely melted. Season with salt.

The curd will thicken as it cools; it should be spreadable, like a jam. Once it is completely cooled, you can slather it on the cake. I like to store the extra curd in an old jam or mason jar in the fridge; it will last about a week or so.

Simple Whipped Cream

1 cup (236 ml) heavy whipping cream, cold

¼ cup (50 g) granulated white sugar

1 tablespoon pure vanilla extract or vanilla bean paste

Chill the mixing bowl for at least 30 minutes before you whip the cream. It will whip up easier when chilled, especially on a hot day.

Using a stand mixer with a whisk attachment or an electric handheld mixer, pour in the heavy cream and whisk on high speed for about 3 or 4 minutes until the cream begins to form soft peaks. Keep an eye on it, as it does whip quickly when the bowl is chilled.

Once you have soft peaks and it looks like soft clouds, add the sugar and vanilla extract or paste. Whip for another minute and taste. It should be firm yet creamy.

Place the bowl of whipped cream back into the fridge until you are ready to assemble the cake.

COCONUT COOKIE ICE CREAM SANDWICHES

Makes 6 ice cream sandwiches

2 cups (240 g) all-purpose flour

1 cup (113 g) unsweetened coconut
flakes

¼ teaspoon kosher salt

1 teaspoon baking soda

1 teaspoon baking powder

½ cup (50 g) old fashioned oats

1 cup (16 tablespoons) unsalted butter,
softened

¾ cup (150 g) granulated white sugar

2 eggs, room temperature

1 tablespoon pure vanilla extract

½ cup (85 g) semi-dark chocolate
chips

Vanilla bean ice cream

Optional: toasted coconut (either
unsweetened or sweetened)

When school was out for the summer, we would stop by the local general store to pick out a yummy frozen treat. I always chose the soft and chewy chocolate chip ice cream sandwiches, and I savored every bite on the drive back home. They hold a childhood nostalgia. I recall carefree and blissful memories when I eat them. I couldn't think of a more appropriate dessert for a breezy get-together by the water. I gave those general store cookie sandwiches a coconut update, and they are surprisingly easy to make.

Gather a large mixing bowl and combine the flour, coconut flakes, salt, baking soda, baking powder, and oats. Set aside.

In a stand mixer with a paddle attachment or large bowl with a hand mixer, cream together on medium speed the butter and sugar until smooth. Scrape down the sides of the bowl if necessary.

Crack in both eggs and add the vanilla. Continue to mix at low speed until the eggs are incorporated.

Gently add in the dry ingredients and slowly mix on low speed, scraping down the sides until thoroughly incorporated into a semi-firm dough.

Preheat the oven to 350°F and gather one parchment-lined baking sheet.

Remove the paddle and place the dough bowl directly into the freezer to chill for 30 minutes.

Once the dough is chilled, use a tablespoon and scoop out 2 spoonfuls of dough, roughly 75 g each.

Roll the dough into your hands to form a smooth ball. Gently press the ball down into an even patty as if making a small burger, about ½" thick. Round out the edges to form a smooth and even circle about 2" in diameter and place them on the parchment-lined baking sheet.

Continue to form the cookies until you have at least 10–12 cookies to form even pairs.

Bake the cookies for 12 minutes until the edges are lightly brown and remove them onto a cookie rack to cool completely.

Meanwhile prepare the chocolate sauce by filling a small saucepan with a few inches of water. Place a glass mixing bowl on top so it fits snuggly without the bottom touching the water.

Bring the water to a low simmer and add the chocolate chips to the glass bowl.

Gently stir the chocolate chips together until they completely melt into a smooth, velvety sauce. Turn off the heat and remove the chocolate bowl from the pot.

For easy clean-up, gather a small quart Ziploc bag and spoon the melted chocolate into the bag.

Make a tiny snip with scissors at one of the corners of the bag for piping the chocolate drizzle.

Working quickly, drizzle one or two diagonal layers of melted chocolate across the tops of the cookies on the rack. For an even finish, start off the edge of the cookie and smoothly finish over the other end of the cookie without stopping in a fluid motion.

Once the tops of the cookies are drizzled, place them onto a large platter into the freezer to set completely for at least one hour.

Once the chocolate on the cookies is set, scoop two tablespoons of ice cream onto one cookie. It's easier to spread the ice cream if it is not frozen solid. If you're having trouble spreading it in a single layer, let the ice cream rest at room temperature until it's slightly creamier. Sandwich it together with a second cookie and run a spoon or knife around the sides of the ice cream to smooth it out.

When one sandwich is completed, I place it back onto a plate in the freezer until I'm finished assembling them all. They will melt quickly if left out too long.

If you'd like to add the extra bit of coconut, simply toast a handful of coconut in a skillet over low heat until golden, stirring constantly to prevent burning. Once you sandwich it together with ice cream, dab the toasted coconut around the sides of the sandwich.

Either serve them immediately or let them chill in the freezer for 30 minutes to firm up. If you wrap them well with plastic wrap and seal them in a freezer bag, they will last up to two weeks.

SUMMER BERRIES IN LEMON SYRUP WITH BUTTERMILK BISCUITS

Serves 6

2 lbs (900 g) mixed berries, such
    as strawberries, blackberries,
    blueberries, raspberries, mulberries
½ cup (100 grams) granulated white
    sugar
Juice of one large lemon
1 tablespoon lemon zest
Kosher salt
Edible flowers, such as chamomile,
    violets, primroses, or nasturtiums
Fresh mint

Options to serve with:
Whipped cream
Vanilla bean ice cream
Pistachio gelato
Whipped mascarpone
Plain Greek full-fat yogurt
Ricotta

Midsummer visits to a local berry farm in Vermont to pick strawberries, raspberries, and blackberries are a family tradition. For us, nearly every dessert consists of plump berries in the summertime, especially on the 4th of July. Sweet berries macerated in a lemony sugary syrup on top of buttermilk biscuits honor the berry bounty, whether wild or from the local farm stand or farmers market. This dessert is a variation of the quintessential and beloved strawberry shortcake that has adorned our outdoor table for many idyllic summers.

Hull the strawberries and cut them into quarters or halves, depending on how large they are.

Combine all the berries with the sugar, lemon juice, lemon zest, and a pinch of kosher salt in a large bowl.

Let the berries sit in the lemon syrup for at least one hour. They also can be set in the fridge for a day, and they will be perfectly fine.

Serve a generous portion of the berries on top of a scoop of creamy ice cream with a crisp biscotti or between a halved buttermilk biscuit (recipe follows). Sprigs of mint and little edible flower blossoms such as chamomile or nasturtiums add a whimsical flourish.

Sweet Buttermilk Biscuits

Makes 10 biscuits

3 cups (360 g) all-purpose flour

3 teaspoons baking powder

¼ teaspoon baking soda

1 tablespoon light golden-brown sugar

1 teaspoon kosher salt

8 tablespoons cold unsalted butter, cut into small chunks

1 cup (236 ml) cold buttermilk plus 2 tablespoons

Turbinado sugar for sprinkling

Preheat the oven to 425°F. Prepare a baking sheet lined with parchment paper.

In a large mixing bowl, combine the flour, baking powder, baking soda, sugar, and salt. You can use a large food processor as well.

Using a pastry cutter, add the butter chunks to the bowl or food processor until they resemble pea-sized crumbs in the flour mixture. If using a food processor, pulse a few times until the mixture resembles coarse crumbs. Remove the mixture from the food processor and into a large mixing bowl.

Pour in the buttermilk and gently stir with a wooden spoon until the mixture comes together.

Using your hands, place the rough dough onto a lightly floured work surface. Gently bring the dough together and use an additional tablespoon of buttermilk if needed. Pat the dough in your hands and shape it into about a rough 8" square, about ½" thick. Be careful not to overwork the dough because it will make the final biscuit too solid and not as flaky. Once you have a rough rectangle, wrap it in plastic wrap and place it in the freezer for 30 minutes or the fridge for an hour. In the meantime, you can prepare the berries or cream.

Once the dough is chilled, place the dough back on the lightly floured work surface and gather a 3" scalloped biscuit cutter, although you can decide how large you'd like them to be. Cut out as many biscuits as you can, place them on the baking sheet, and gently reshape and repeat the process with the remaining dough.

In a small bowl, pour in a tablespoon or two of buttermilk, and using a pastry brush or your fingers, lightly brush the tops of each biscuit with a dab of the buttermilk. Sprinkle a dash of turbinado sugar on top of each.

Bake the biscuits for 15–20 minutes until the tops are lightly golden brown.

To assemble the biscuits with the sugary berries, split each warm biscuit in half. Add a dollop of whipped cream, vanilla ice cream, or whipped mascarpone on one half. Add a generous spoonful of the berries with some sweet juice on top of the cream. Top if off with the remaining biscuit half with more berries on the side.

SKILLET BROWNIE WITH CHERRIES & WALNUTS

Serves 6–8

16 tablespoons unsalted butter

1½ cups (126 g) unsweetened cocoa powder

1 teaspoon (5 g) kosher salt

1 teaspoon (3 g) baking powder

2 cups (396 g) granulated white sugar

3 eggs

1 tablespoon vanilla extract

1½ cups (204 g) all-purpose flour

⅓ cup (79 ml) heavy whipping cream

1 generous handful of halved and pitted cherries

½ cup (52 g) chopped walnuts

¼ cup (20 g) sweetened coconut

1.5 oz (45 g) 70% dark chocolate chunks

Maldon salt

For campfire nights and backyard cookouts, this skillet brownie is decadent, rich, and oh so heavenly. It's a quick bake for something so satisfying with juicy cherries, chocolate chunks, crunchy walnuts, and sweet coconut. If you're with close company, set the skillet right on the table, hand out spoons for everyone to dig in, and share with vanilla ice cream around the fire.

Preheat the oven to 350°F. Gather a 9"–10.5" cast iron pre-seasoned skillet.

Over medium-low heat, slowly melt the butter, swirling it in the pan to coat the sides evenly. Turn off the heat once the butter is fully melted and set aside.

Combine the cocoa powder, salt, baking powder, and sugar in a medium-sized mixing bowl.

Add the cocoa mixture to the melted butter in the skillet and roughly combine them with a rubber spatula.

Pour in the vanilla and crack in the eggs and gently whisk them in to the batter until thoroughly combined.

Add the flour to the batter and slowly mix it with a rubber spatula until smooth and even. Be careful as you stir so the flour doesn't run over the skillet edges.

Slowly pour in the heavy cream and gradually stir the batter together until it is smooth and glossy.

Reserve a few of the cherries, walnuts, coconut, and chocolate chunks for the topping before adding them into the batter, gently incorporating them with a rubber spatula.

Scatter the reserved cherries, walnuts, coconut, and chocolate chunks on top. Sprinkle with a pinch of Maldon salt over the top evenly.

Bake for the brownie for 10 minutes and then cover it with aluminum foil to prevent the coconut from over-browning. Continue to bake for another 10–12 minutes until the edges are bubbly and the center is still a little fudgy. When you insert a knife, it should come out a little streaky but not raw batter. It will continue to cook once you remove it from the oven. I like it undercooked rather than overdone!

Dig into the brownie with a big spoon when it's warm with a scoop or two of vanilla bean or your choice of ice cream on top.

SPICED WINTER SQUASH CAKE

Serves 6–8

2 cups (240 g) all-purpose flour

2 teaspoons ground cinnamon

1 teaspoon kosher salt

1 teaspoon baking soda

½ teaspoon ground nutmeg

Pinch of ground cloves

4 eggs

1¾ cups (363 g) light golden-brown
sugar

1 cup (236 ml) vegetable oil

1 cup (212 g) unsweetened butternut
squash purée (you can use sugar
pumpkin, acorn, or kabocha)

1 heaping tablespoon orange zest

1 tablespoon pure vanilla extract

1 8-oz (226 g) package cream cheese,
softened

½ cup (50 g) powdered sugar

¼ cup (59 ml) Vermont maple syrup

1 cup (113 g) chopped walnuts

On a chilly autumn day, this spiced winter squash cake is a delicious treat for a cozy gathering. It's ochre hue and earthy sweetness celebrates the harvest and seasonal shift. Gather some wooly blankets and invite over some friends for hot tea or coffee and a thick slice of this cake on a brisk September evening.

Preheat the oven to 350°F and grease and line an 8" x 8" baking tin with parchment paper.

Combine the flour, cinnamon, salt, baking soda, nutmeg, and cloves in a large mixing bowl.

In a stand mixer with a paddle attachment or large bowl using a handheld mixer, crack in the eggs and add the sugar, vegetable oil, butternut squash purée, orange zest, and vanilla. Mix the ingredients until it is a smooth and even consistency, about 2–3 minutes.

Gently spoon the dry ingredients into the mixing bowl and continue to mix at medium speed until the batter is smooth and even. Scrape down the sides of the bowl several times to ensure the dry ingredients are properly incorporated.

Pour the batter into the baking tin and bake for 30–35 minutes until an inserted knife comes out clean.

Allow the cake to cool completely on a wire rack before frosting. To make the frosting, whisk together, either by hand or in a stand mixer, the cream cheese, powdered sugar, and maple syrup until it is creamy and no lumps remain.

Gently spread the frosting on top of the cake in an even layer. Sprinkle the chopped walnuts over the frosting with additional fresh orange zest.

COCKTAILS

There's reason to celebrate with something bubbly and refreshing when the weather is glorious. A crisp glass of white or rosé pairs nearly with every summery dish. Although, when I feel like mixing up a little something different, an effervescent cocktail (like the following recipes) adds a little pep and cheer. Not every get-together needs a mixed drink on the menu, but when it feels right, cheers to that. I've also included a few nonalcoholic versions, which are bright and equally refreshing options, such as the sweet basil lemonade—a perfect drink to beat the July heat. Whatever you choose, be it iced tea, pinot grigio, or the honeydew agua fresca on page 197, be sure it is cold with plenty to go around!

SOLSTICE SPRITZ

Makes 1 cocktail

Juice of ½ a grapefruit

1 oz Aperol

3 oz sparkling rosé

Splash lime seltzer

Fresh rosemary sprig

Grapefruit wedge

Reminiscent of a classic Aperol Spritz, this is a vibrant and sparkling cocktail to welcome the summer season. Its gorgeous ruddy coral color is the sunset's radiance in a glass. Sip and savor the longest day of the year!

In your serving glass, add several cubes of ice.

Squeeze the grapefruit half into the glass.

Pour in the Aperol and top off with sparkling rosé and a splash of lime seltzer.

Garnish with a fresh rosemary sprig and grapefruit wedge.

HONEYDEW & MINT AGUA FRESCA

Serves 4–6

1.5 lb (600g) honeydew melon, peeled, deseeded, and cut into small chunks
1 small handful fresh mint leaves
Juice 4 limes
3 750-ml bottles sparkling water
Lime rounds to garnish

During Maui's sweltering summers, I'm always looking for refreshing and creative ways to perk up an ordinary pitcher of water. Infusing water with fresh fruit is by no means revolutionary, but this one is a keeper with sweet honeydew and lime. It's cooling, energizing, and a sprightly color too!

In a large blender, add the honeydew, mint leaves, lime juice, and one bottle of sparkling water. Blend until smooth and puréed. You may have to work in batches depending on the size of your blender.

Strain the liquid through a fine-mesh sieve into your serving pitcher.

Pour in the remaining two bottles of sparkling water with ample ice.

Add in the additional lime rounds, a few sprigs of mint, and serve chilled.

POMELO PALOMA

Makes 6 cocktails

3 tablespoons turbinado or coarse
  sugar

2 teaspoons pomelo zest

2 oz blue agave

2 oz water

A handful of rosemary sprigs

12 oz freshly squeezed pomelo juice

Juice of 5 limes

8 oz blanco tequila

1 375 ml bottle brut rosé

3–4 limes, sliced into rounds

Pomelo peels to garnish

If a margarita and a paloma had an affair, this cocktail would be the blushing babe. It's cheerful, fun, and illuminates in the summer sun. Pomelos are generally less bitter than grapefruit, although if they're hard to find (or too shy to ask to pick one from a neighbor's tree), grapefruit is a widely available alternative too. Stemless wine glasses or mason jars work just fine to serve on a lovely tray.

On a small plate, combine the sugar and pomelo zest.

Run a lime wedge along the rim of the glasses and then dip the rim into the sugar mix, coating a fine sugar line around the top of each glass.

To make the rosemary syrup, add the agave, water, and one rosemary sprig to a small saucepan over medium heat. Whisk the agave into the water until completely dissolved and slightly thickened. Remove the rosemary and turn off the heat.

Gather a large pitcher and pour in the pomelo juice, lime juice, and tequila. Give it a quick stir and gather your glasses.

Fill ¼ of each glass with ice cubes and pour in the pomelo mix, dividing it evenly between the 6 glasses.

Top off each glass a generous splash of brut rosé.

Garnish with rosemary sprigs, lime rounds, and pomelo peels.

BASIL LEMONADE

Serves 4–6

1 large handful of basil, plus more to
  garnish
⅔ cup (140 g) granulated white sugar
4½ cups (1064 ml) water
6 large lemons (reserve 1 for strips)

When I was young, I used to have a lemonade stand with my sister and best friend every 4th of July, which was a success, if I might add. That old summer classic gets an update with the addition of sweet basil. It's a quite wonderfully unexpected flavor on the first sip, but that little note of peppery basil is so refreshing, you'll want to make two batches. Think of it as another creative way to use up all that basil in the summer garden!

Combine the basil and sugar in a small bowl. Lightly muddle them just until the basil is slightly worn down.

Add the sugared basil to a small saucepan and peel the rind of one lemon into thin strips and place it into the pan with ½ cup of water.

Bring the basil syrup to a low boil for about 3–5 minutes until the basil is broken down and the sugar is dissolved. Let the syrup sit for 10 minutes off the heat. Strain the syrup and set it in the fridge for at least 30 minutes.

In your serving pitcher, pour in basil syrup, 4 cups of water, and the juice of the remaining 5 lemons.

Taste and add additional sugar or lemon juice depending on your preference, I like it just shy of lip-smacking tart. Serve with ice, lemon slices, and an additional small handful of basil leaves in the pitcher.

LILLET SANGRIA WITH BLOOD ORANGES & PLUMS

Serves 6

2 blood oranges, thinly sliced[3]

2 red plums, pitted and thinly sliced

1 small navel orange, thinly sliced

1 750 ml bottle sauvignon blanc, chilled

1 750 ml bottle Lillet, chilled

1 handful fresh mint

Optional: sparkling orange soda (San Pellegrino Blood Orange) or dry prosecco

Sangria is a fantastic choice for a lively and lush evening with friends. The juicer the fruit, the better! Lillet is a fruity and delicate aperitif that is a sweet accompaniment to a crisp sauvignon blanc. The sunset hues remind me of the stunning shows that paint the Maui sky.

In a large serving pitcher, add half of the fruit slices and half of both bottles of sauvignon blanc and Lillet. Gently stir and chill in the fridge for at least one hour.

When you are ready to serve, add in the rest of the fruit slices, mint, and pour in the remaining sauvignon blanc and Lillet. For optional fizz, top off each poured drink with either a splash of sparkling orange soda or prosecco. Gently stir with a long spoon and serve chilled. I prefer not to use ice as it gets too watery, especially on a humid day.

For a nonalcoholic version for the little ones, simply use San Pellegrino Blood Orange soda with the fruit slices and mint on ice.

» *3 Since the recipe isn't served on ice, you can freeze the second half of the fruit slices beforehand if you like and add them in once you're ready to serve.*

MENU PAIRINGS

An Early Summer Brunch

Crème Fraîche Dip with crudité platter
A Buttery Green Salad
Goat Cheese & Rainbow Chard Frittata
Oh, Là Là Tiramisu
Pomelo Paloma

Casual Family Get Together

A Simple Fresh Salsa
Sweet Pepper Wild Rice Salad
Prosciutto-Wrapped Chicken Skewers
    with Fresh Pesto
Summer Berries in Lemon Syrup with
    Buttermilk Biscuits
Basil Lemonade

Backyard Barbecue

Grilled Romaine & Radicchio Salad
Grilled Strip Steak with Hawaiian Coffee Rub
Herb Potato Salad with Green
    Beans & Lemon
Skillet Brownie with Cherries & Walnuts
Honeydew & Mint Agua Fresca

Summer Soirée

Grilled Oysters with Herb & Lemon Butter
Stone Fruit Panzanella
Coastal Linguine with Clams
Pistachio & Cherry Affogato
Solstice Spritz

Garden's Bounty

Bruschetta with Summer Garden Caponata
Swiss Chard & Cannellini Bean Dip
Stone Fruit Panzanella
Summer Garden Orecchiette Pasta Salad
Strawberry & Peach Crisp

La Vita è Dolce

Bruschetta with Heirloom Tomatoes with
    Basil & Buffalo Mozzarella
Burrata with Melon & Prosciutto
Coastal Linguine with Clams
Pistachio & Cherry Affogato

Summer Smorgasbord

A Simple Fresh Salsa
Grilled Sausage Smorgasbord
Vermont Backroad Baked Beans
Skillet Brownie with Cherries & Walnuts

A Mediterranean Holiday

Baked Feta with Olives & Cherry Tomatoes
A Better Caprese
Sicilian Tuna Spaghetti
Whipped Mascarpone with Strawberries
    & Amaretto
Solstice Spritz

A Taste of Maui

Garden Green Beans with Chili & Almonds
Winslow's Sweet Buns
Maui Mahi-Mahi Burger
Tropics Slaw
Honey & Mint Agua Fresca
Coconut Ice Cream Sandwiches

A Vegetarian's Delight

Off-the-Vine Gazpacho
Cucumber, Orange & Watercress Salad
  with Caraway
Spinach & Dandelion Pie with
  Golden Raisins & Pine Nuts
Lemon Sponge Cake with Fresh Lemon Curd
Basil Lemonade

An Autumnal Feast

Baked Camembert in a Sourdough Boule
Roasted Beet & Arugula Salad
Butternut Squash & Apple Lasagna with
  Béchamel Sauce
Spiced Winter Squash Cake

A Midsummer's Night

Bruschetta with Roasted Cherries with
  Gorgonzola, Honey, & Thyme
Stone Fruit Panzanella
Caramelized Red Onion & Fennel Tart
Kula Blackberry Tart
Lillet Sangria with Blood Oranges & Plums

Pizza Party

A Different Caprese
Grilled Romaine & Radicchio Salad
Grilled Flatbread
Skillet Brownie with Cherries & Walnuts

Light & Fresh

Crème Fraîche Dip with Garden Herbs
A Buttery Green Salad
Pearl Couscous with Grilled Shrimp &
  Summer Veggies
Grapefruit & Rosemary Cheesecake

Homestead Favorites

Baked Feta with Olives & Cherry Tomatoes
Garden Green Beans with Chili & Almonds
Roast Chicken Thighs with Figs,
  Olives, & Lemon
Farm Stand Strawberry & Peach Crisp
Basil Lemonade

An August Afternoon

Off-the-Vine Gazpacho
Garden Green Beans with Chili & Almonds
Grilled Flatbread
Whipped Mascarpone with Strawberries
  & Amaretto
Honeydew & Mint Agua Fresca

ACKNOWLEDGMENTS

This creative journey that I find myself on is without a doubt indebted to a special few. I am ever so grateful to my parents, who were the supportive force behind this book. It wouldn't have been possible without their belief in me and my work. It has been invaluable and given me the courage to pursue a happy and meaningful career. Little did I know that all the outdoor dinner parties we hosted at our lovely home would be the foundation for this book. I feel so blessed to have had the privilege of growing up on a farm centered on our outdoor table. Thank you to my mother especially, whose creativity and artistry provided encouraging feedback and help, particularly recreating a summer table on a cold November day in Vermont!

My siblings, Olivia and Liam, are also owed many thanks for their constant support and cheers along the sidelines. Their faith in me has given me the confidence to soldier on and follow my dreams.

A special thank you to my agent Jessica Alvarez, who was the first to believe in my work from the very beginning. Who knew we would be going around together for a second time!

Of course, a warm thanks to Lisa McGuinness at Mango Publishing, who proposed this wonderful book to me. I am so fortunate to have this opportunity to write another.

Thank you to the many friends who have added their input and taste-tested my many failed recipe attempts with unwavering support.

You all will forever have a seat at my outdoor table!

AUTHOR BIOGRAPHY

Alanna is a photographer based in Maui, Hawaii, originally from the green mountains of Vermont. Her work celebrates seasonality and outdoor living. Her first book, *The Art of Picnics,* inspired *The Outdoor Table.* She currently lives in an upcountry cottage in Maui with her sweet pup Winslow.

yellow pear 🍐 press

Yellow Pear Press, established in 2015, publishes inspiring, charming, clever, distinctive, playful, imaginative, beautifully designed lifestyle books, cookbooks, literary fiction, notecards, and journals with a certain joie de vivre in both content and style. Yellow Pear Press books have been honored by the Independent Publisher Book (IPPY) Awards, National Indie Excellence Awards, Independent Press Awards, and International Book Awards. Reviews of our titles have appeared in Kirkus Reviews, Foreword Reviews, Booklist, Midwest Book Review, San Francisco Chronicle, and New York Journal of Books, among others. Yellow Pear Press joined forces with Mango Publishing in 2020, both with the vision to continue publishing clever and innovative books. The fact that they're both named after fruit is a total coincidence.

We love hearing from our readers, so please stay in touch with us and follow us at:

Facebook: Mango Publishing
Twitter: @MangoPublishing
Instagram: @MangoPublishing
LinkedIn: Mango Publishing
Pinterest: Mango Publishing

Newsletter: mangopublishinggroup.com/newsletter